ALASKA CRUISE

with the Cruise Addict's Wife

Deb Graham

You'll LOVE Alaska!
Deb G

Alaska Cruise With The Cruise Addict's Wife

Copyright 2017 All Rights Reserved.

No part or portion of this book may be copied or disseminated without express written permission of the author, who holds all rights and doesn't share well.

Other Books by Deb Graham

Tips From The Cruise Addict's Wife

More Tips From The Cruise Addict's Wife

Murder On Deck a *cruise novel*

Peril In Paradise a *cruise novel*

Mediterranean Cruise With The Cruise Addict's Wife

How To Write Your Story

How To Complain...*and get what you deserve*

Hungry Kids Campfire Cookbook

Kid Food On A Stick

Quick and Clever Kids' Crafts

Awesome Science Experiments for Kids

Savory Mug Cooking

Uncommon Household Tips

Why Cruise to Alaska?

What are you waiting for?

So many decisions!

What kind of people go to Alaska?

When to go to Alaska

Which month is best?

Which Cruise Line Is Right For You?

What kind of cabin is best in Alaska?

What is there to do in Alaska?

Private Tours

Traditional/Local Foods

Glaciers—it's Alaska, after all!

Weather

What to buy in Alaska?

Embarkation Ports:

Cruise Ports And What To Do There

Wildlife

Birds

Sea Creatures and Whales

Dolphins and Porpoises

What To Pack

Why Cruise to Alaska?

I can sum up my advice about cruising to Alaska quite succinctly: if you get the chance to go, <u>*GO*</u>. **Just go!** Read the rest of this book anyway, but that sums it up.

I've traveled a lot. I've visited all fifty United State extensively, as well as close to thirty countries, yet, Alaska calls me back. Forget San Francisco: I left my heart the first time I stepped on Alaska's soil and I go back to visit my body part as often as I can manage.

If you've read my other cruise books - and you surely should, so you don't miss anything!- you already know I'm married to the Cruise Addict. He earned that title on our first cruise, a cruise to Alaska to celebrate our twentieth anniversary. He balked at going, and I do mean *balked!* We live about two hours from the port, and he verbally dug his heels in the whole drive there. He was quite clear, and quite vocal, that he was going to hate, *hate,* **<u>hate</u>** cruising, and hate Alaska even more. But within hours of gazing at the scenery of the Inside Passage, he was hooked, complete with hook, line and sinker...and a full-feathered cruise addiction was born.

Since then, I've been on dozens of once-in-a-lifetime cruises with the Cruise Addict, and quite a few of them have been to Alaska. Something about our nation's 50th state pulls me back, over and over. It could be the wildness, the people, the scenery, the sheer vastness; Alaska's one my very favorite places!

But why should *you* consider a cruise to Alaska? For one thing, you'd be in good company. Alaska has grabbed the cruise market in a big way. It's currently one of the most-booked cruise destinations in the world, second only to the Caribbean (and it's not a fair comparison, since Alaska's cruise season is much shorter) Alaska is in bold print on many people's bucket lists. But why?

Alaska isn't like anywhere else in the world. The fiftieth state is big, for starters. If you overlay a map of Alaska on a map of the mainland United States, you'll see its boundaries stretch from California to the Carolinas all the way to Canada. We're talking big, *really* big, bigger than Montana, Texas, and California combined. You could fit Washington State, where I live, into Alaska nine times with land left over.

A few more facts? Alaska has the most northern point (Point Barrow) and the most western point (Cape Wrangell is further west than Hawaii) in the whole United States. Florida is known for its thousands of lakes (many with resident alligators), but Alaska has eight times more inland water than Florida. Florida is also known for its long coastline, over 1,350 miles of coast, but Alaska leaves it in the dust, boasting fully fifty percent of the entire U.S. coastline, nearly 6,640 miles long. And not a single sandy sun-bathable beach to be found!

If Alaska has no warm, tropical beaches with palm trees, what's the point of a cruise? In the Caribbean, beach play and sunbathing are major activities, while Old World Europe is for history. New England and the Maritimes draw tourists to see "the colors" as the autumn leaves turn. In Alaska, it's all about the great land itself.

Alaska boasts more glaciers than anywhere else except the Antarctic and Greenland. The highest peaks in North America are in Alaska, and are they stunning! Lynn Canal is the deepest fjord on the continent. Alaska's population density is so far less per mile than anywhere else in America, it hardly registers as density at all. With no big-city industries, the air is so fresh, your lungs will purr. The people...the silence...the pristine scenery...the frontier spirit...oh, I do love Alaska!

There's a wildness, a pioneering spirit, which lingers long after the last major gold rush faded into history. The people who live in Alaska year round are fiercely proud of their culture, and not really interested in outside influences tainting their way of life. That's not to say they're backwoods, by any means: Alaskan students are typically academically a year or more ahead of their peers in the lower Forty-Eight. With class sizes averaging around ten students (in some villages, less than that), they rely heavily on technology, including holding class discussions on the internet, live.

That's interesting, but what's in it for you? What exactly is the Alaska experience? It's wilderness, small towns with a can-do spirit you won't find anywhere else. It's snow-capped mountains and glaciers calving and gold panning in any stream you see. It's the best way to step off of the stressful hamster-wheel that is modern workday life.

What else will you experience in Alaska?

Glaciers! There are 617 officially named glaciers in Alaska, and the unnamed estimate reaches close to one hundred thousand. Depending on your cruise itinerary, you'll get up close and personal with one or more of the massive tidewater glaciers: Glacier Bay, Hubbard Glacier, Sawyer Glacier in Tracy Arm Fjord, Mendenhall Glacier, or the twin glaciers at College Fjord. Plus, ice fields and smaller glaciers are visible on nearly every peak the ship passes. "Small" is a relative term; some of the glaciers are bigger than your hometown, with ranch-house-sized chunks calving often. And the color...that blue trapped for hundreds of years in the compressed ice rivals any old Caribbean beach. Well, wait a minute; I am rather fond of the Caribbean blue waters.

Wilderness! No big-city lights in Alaska, but you can soak up the spirit of the land with hiking, boating, fishing, floatplane trips, walking on glaciers, white-water rafting, sea kayaking, or lazy meandering at your own pace into some of the most beautiful areas you'll ever see, with silence so thick, you can feel it.

Mountains! Seven of North America's tallest mountains are located in Alaska and the Yukon, and you can see some of them right from your cruise ship. If you want even greater heights, add a land tour to Denali, North America's largest mountain, onto your cruise literary.

History! There aren't any Old World Cathedrals or ancient ruins in Alaska, but don't discount the rich history here. Native American history is the living variety, preserved and ongoing in art, food, dance, language, and did I mention totem poles?

If you do crave ancient works, seek out the petroglyphs in various places in Alaska. At least a couple of thousand years old, they certainly qualify as Old. They're not hard to find, and you won't faint in the heat getting to see them, as I nearly did in southern Utah, hiking up to the Anasazi petroglyphs in 115-degree heat. The biggest shade was cast by a puny sagebrush. However, I did learn that old Indian trick of holding a pebble in one's mouth when there's no water to be had actually helped. Okay, it was a fruit chew, not a dirty old pebble, but you get the idea. And I did take water, lest you think I'm that foolish; the little grandsons needed it more than I.

The gold rush wasn't long ago at all. The gold-fevered 49ers, Sam McGee, Soapy Smith, Joe Juneau...Alaska is the place of legends! Feel free to join in; just last month I saw people working a portable gold-gathering sluice in a stream, disdaining the nine-to-five grind. That little pouch of gold flecks is a mighty satisfying way to wrap up the day's work.

Silence! Once you walk a few blocks from any port in Alaska, you'll find yourself transported back to a simpler time, a quieter pace. Go further into the wilderness, and the silence becomes tangible. It's easy to imagine how it was a hundred years ago, because in a lot of Alaska, it's still that way. There are still parts of Alaska where humans have never walked, where the nearest city is several days away, where the old ways of life are simply the day-to-day way of life.

Wildlife! It's common to spot moose, caribou, Dall sheep, grizzly bears, puffin, bald eagles, porcupines, seals, humpbacks and orcas, gray whales and musk ox, and perhaps even the largest mammal on earth, the blue whale, all in their natural habitat. Interacting and observing Nature in her glory will change your life. There's a whole section on wildlife later on.

A few other advantages of a trip to Alaska: Crime is low, overall, making it a safe place to visit. Just keep your wits about you and mind your steps. And because it's part of America, language won't be a barrier, currency is familiar, and you can easily ship a box home if you purchase a too-large-to-pack souvenir.

What are you waiting for?

But is a cruise the best way to see Alaska? For a good overview of the coastal cities and tidewater glaciers, a cruise can't be beat. You'd spend many times more to fly to each port city. Add in lodging and meals in each place, and a cruise is a better bargain by the minute. Yes, you can't explore every mile of the Great Land by cruise ship, but you can sure get a good taste of it.

What draws nearly two million tourists to Alaska every year? The scenery and once-in-a-lifetime experiences alone are worth the trip. There's an atmosphere, a pioneering spirit that lingers long after the last major gold rush faded into history. The people who live there year round are fiercely proud of their heritage and culture, and many are eager to share it through dance, song, cultural exchanges, and living history. And it's a wonderful thing to see wild animals in their habitat, when *you're* the visitor!

Why should you see Alaska now? Most visitors find it utterly life-changing, unlike any other vacation. There's something soul-soothing about lingering on deck under the Northern Lights or spending an entire afternoon watching glaciers calving, admiring orcas leaping though ice floes over an elegant dinner. Sure, you can eat fish at home, but a fresh Alaskan salmon can't be beat.

Another good reason to see Alaska soon is that it may not last forever, at least in its current state. Climate change is real; ask any Alaskan. Whether you subscribe to the man-influenced-global-warming dogma or simply the natural-cycles-of-the-earth theory, Alaska's landscape is changing, and it's changing visibly.

At Exit Glacier outside Seward, sign posts with years marked on them line the path of the glacier's receding path. It's about a hundred ninety feet every year. Some tidewater glaciers, including Portage Glacier, have receded so much, they no longer reach the water's edge at all. In other places, glaciers surge forward faster than in any recorded time. Tracy Arm showcases the twin Sawyer Glaciers, pushing forward so fast, it's estimated the lovely blue fjord on the north will be a deep lake in just a few short years. This is a trip you just can't put off a few decades!

So many decisions!

While some cruises begin in San Francisco or San Diego, leap-frogging up the west coast, most Alaska cruises begin and or end in Seattle or Vancouver, BC, or Anchorage. I'll discuss pros and cons of each in a little bit. For now, know that round-trip and one-way cruises are most common. Round trip takes passengers from a port and returns to the same city at the end of the cruise, usually Seattle or Vancouver. One way cruises are either northbound or southbound, beginning in either Vancouver or Seattle and ending in Anchorage's ports, or vice versa. Both have distinct advantages.

Due to distance, there are no 3-4 day cruises to Alaska. It's not like Florida, where you can hop a weekend booze-cruise and call it good. You want time to see the place, after waiting so long to visit the Great Land! Besides, Alaska is far, farther than you might think. It's as far from Seattle to Anchorage as it is from Boston to Las Vegas! This is not a weekend jaunt.

Alaska cruises can be anywhere from seven to twenty-eight days, depending on itinerary. Most run seven days long, either one way or round trip from Seattle or Vancouver, or north- or southbound from Anchorage or Vancouver. It's totally up to you. Later on, I'll help you sort out which itinerary and cruise line will suit you best.

On top of the cruise, which is glorious on its own, you can extend the experience by adding a land tour to the beginning or end of your cruise. Piggybacking from the cruise ship onto a motor coach or train, you can head inland to Denali, national parks, small inland towns, clear up to Fairbanks if you so choose.

Are you up to so much adventure? Of course, encountering a moose on a hike or an otter by kayak is thrilling, but for the less adventurous or able-bodied, the wildlife viewing from the deck of your ship is equally satisfying. As a bonus, most, if not all Alaska itineraries include scenic cruising days where your sole intention is to whip out the binoculars, grab a cup of hot cocoa and scour the horizon for any sign of a whale fluke or bald eagle's white head.

If you can reach out and touch an iceberg or come within feet of a brown bear fishing for salmon, I'd call that pretty up close and personal. In Alaska, there's an abundance of glowing blue glaciers and wild animals patrolling the land, air and sea -- and you can see them from the comfort of your cruise ship.

Factor in itinerary it's probably the most important consideration in planning an Alaskan cruise. You know your style of travel better than anyone. Some cruise lines spend only a half day in the place you've always wanted to see. While almost all cruises to Alaska spend at least a couple of hours at a major glacier, it's important to decide which one you'd rather see. Is well-known Glacier Bay on your must-see list? Sawyer is beautiful, and Hubbard one of the most glaciers in the state. Are you most interested in small towns that still have the old Alaskan charm, or do you want a jump-off point to more adventure? Is there a particular tour you've always dreamed of? If it's only offered in one port, make sure your itinerary goes there. Don't glom onto the first cruise you see; take time to weigh what you value most.

One-way or round trip? One-way trips can see more, and go further north, but you'll have to add in the cost of a one-way flight back. Round trip is more of a contained itinerary, tends to cost less, and stays in the calmer waters of the beautiful Inside

Passage a good portion of the time. About two-thirds of all visitors to Alaska opt for the Inside Passage route, while others insist crossing Gulf of Alaska route gives a richer experience.

Let's look at both:

An Inside Passage cruise is typically a round-trip cruise from Seattle or Vancouver and back to the same port. They include stops at three or four port towns, typically Juneau, Skagway, Ketchikan, and either Sitka, Haines, or Victoria. These seven-day cruises usually spend a day in Glacier Bay or Tracy Arm, and a couple days at sea.

There are distinct pros and cons to this choice, as with anything else in your life. Since it's round trip, the ship won't cover as much ground as a one-way itinerary; it's less in-depth. On the other hand, you'll still see highlights of Alaska's coastline, with more of a relaxing, resort-like tempo. If you long to simply relax, sit back and watch coastal scenery go by, while getting a good taste of Alaska, this itinerary will likely suit you just fine. Bonus: round-trip airfare from your home to Seattle or Vancouver is likely less expensive than one-way fare.

Cruises across the Gulf of Alaska sail northbound or southbound between either Vancouver or Seattle and Anchorage's ports of either Whittier or Seward. Itineraries go to most of the same places as a round-trip, plus extras, perhaps Valdez, Hubbard Glacier, College Fjord or one or more other small towns along the way. If you're heart set on adding a land portion to your cruise, this one's for you. Land tours typically take out of Anchorage on their way to places north, and you'll need the head start. Even if you don't add a land tour (half of passengers don't), you may prefer this itinerary just to enjoy more coastline, small towns, and glaciers. But I offer a warning: this is the very itinerary where Husband morphed into the Cruise Addict. Gorgeous!

What kind of people go to Alaska?

What kind of people travel to Alaska? They range in age from infant to elderly, come from all over the planet, and tend to be more active-minded than on some other itineraries. Stick-in-the-muds are generally not attracted to Alaska. I've met people from Germany, New Zealand, China, France, and South Africa, and over forty states, to name a few. Alaska's the place to be, no matter where you're from! Passengers in Alaska aren't there for ancient history or glittery nightlife, although most ships offer at least a taste of that.

Make a point of talking to your fellow adventurers; they're generally happy, engaging, involved people.

Well, there are exceptions. I met a woman on her second cruise to Alaska who raved about the beauty, the scenery, the water, the glaciers, the trees, on and ON.

I finally asked, "Didn't you say you had been here before?"

She sheepishly replied, "Yes, last summer, but I spent all day every day playing Bingo in the theater."

Oh.

She was an odd duck; most folks who go to Alaska are there to really experience it!

Who should you cruise with? We've enjoyed cruises to Alaska with extended family (both sides), our kids, our oldest grandchildren, friends, co-workers, and a few times just Husband and me. A cruise is great for extended families. Each person can do as they please and meet for dinner, or plan tours and port activities all together. In our case, the older generation wanted to play cards in the afternoons with a nap before dinner, the youngest kids loved the children's program, and the young adults and teens partied every night.

One of our best memories was watching our bashful fifteen-month-old granddaughter blossom during her first cruise to Alaska. On Day One, she buried her face in her mother's shoulder anytime a non-family member spoke to her. Within a day, she ventured a soft, "Hi" and within hours she was playing peek-a-boo with the cabin steward. The crew is away from their own families for long months at a stretch, and they doted on her. By Day Four, she carried on full conversations in her baby voice with whoever would make eye contact for more than a moment.

Our waiter brought a fruit plate for her and her big sister as we ordered our dinners, to pass the time while our meal was prepared. The first night, the little one munched all of her grapes and her sister's, too, but shunned the rest of the fruit. Every night after that, the waiter brought a fruit plate for big sister, and a plate of just grapes for the toddler. One of the perks of being a grandparent is that I didn't have to deal with the after-effects in the diapers. That much fruit can't be good!

Our oldest granddaughter cruised to Alaska for the first time with us at the ripe old age of four years. Our dining steward tried to tempt her with the children's menu, but Child was having none of that. Every night, she'd ask us to read the "big people menu" to her, then she'd confidently tell the waiter her order.

  He visibly startled when she asked for two servings of the calamari appetizer. "You won't like it, little princess. Some nice chicken nuggets instead, or a grilled cheese sandwich?"

"No, I want calamari. I like the crunchy tentacles best."

Shaking his head, he complied, then stood a few paces away, watching this pint-sized girl enjoy the fried squid. He didn't argue the next night, just solemnly took her order with everyone else's. Escargot and rigatoni, as I recall.

Where else can your children practice manners and ordering from a menu, and sampling new foods without added cost? If Cutey-Pie decides he doesn't like carpaccio, no harm done. Any passenger, regardless of age, can order from either the children's menu or the regular one, or bounce between the two as they wish. Nothing wrong with prime rib followed by a peachy-weachy sundae.

When to go to Alaska

There are two seasons for Alaska cruising-Shoulder season and Peak season. Shoulder season includes both ends of the cruise line's schedule, generally May, the first week of June, and all of September, plus some lines push back into October now. Peak season is most of June, July and August. Peak season tends to cost more because the weather is better and that's when more people can travel. The kids are out of school, making it easier for families to book a vacation. With demand higher, prices rise, and it's tough to find a good deal. However, if you can travel in shoulder season, when demand is lower, you can take advantage of special promotions and pricing. And don't get fixated on the weather; it's notoriously unpredictable year round, so don't let that stop you!

Each season has advantages and disadvantages. In the early springtime, trees have not leafed out fully, making spotting animals easier. Many animals have their babies in the spring, so you might luck out and see a mama bear with her twins or even triplets, scrounging for breakfast. Winter's snowfall is just starting to melt, making for gorgeous cascading waterfalls from high peaks as the ships glide past. Shining snowfields are abundant higher up. During the school year, ports, as well as ships, tend to be less crowded. Spring wildflowers, baby wildlife, fall foliage and bears feeding for a long winter's nap are things you'll miss at peak season. However, with the weather being somewhat more stable mid-summer, your chances of a tour or excursion being canceled are slim. That can happen pretty often later in the season, especially ones involving flight of any sort.

Though the weather may be a little cooler and wetter in the springtime months, the tourist crowds are smaller, the mosquitoes fewer, and the daylight hours more regular, with no midnight sun to interfere with one's sleeping pattern. The first-of-the-year cruises to Alaska are great!

Summer might have somewhat warmer weather, but you'll pay for it in both higher cruise prices and more crowds. If you insist on traveling mid-summer, you'd be best served making cruise plans well in advance, up to a year or longer. The law of supply and demand applies, and cruise lines take advantage of it. Don't count on bargains, either in the cruise itself or onshore.

Ah, bargains! I have a section later on what to buy—and walk on by— in Alaska. Shopkeepers don't want to have to store unsold goods through the winter months. As the end of the cruise season nears, stores have great sales, up to 90% off. I'm not saying you should book a cruise based on sale prices, but it can't hurt to factor that in your decision-making process. On more than one cruise, it seemed to me every other passenger had the same polar fleece jacket with big, bold sled dog teams along the hem. They probably looked silly wearing it at home, but they were warm, and hey, a bargain is nothing to sneeze at.

Every year, cruise lines tempt Mother Nature by adding a cruise or two at the end of the calendar, hoping to squeeze in one more trip before the towns roll up the sidewalks for winter's quiet season. Fall has some real advantages. Salmon spawn in late summer into autumn, and their struggle to make it to their home base through rivers and streams is breathtaking to see. Often, it looks like there are more fish than water in a stream. It almost seems one could cross the stream and not even get one's feet wet, there are so many fish! Eagles swoop to gorge on the hapless salmon, ignoring tourists with fancy cameras. Bears prepare for their long winter's nap by consuming as many salmon as they can stuff in their faces, one of the few times spotting several bears at once is possible. Amid the frenzy of nature's charges preparing for winter, the ports in Alaska seem to breathe easier once the swarming crowds of summer are past.

Let's look at each month individually.

Which month is best?

The cruise season starts mid-May, so let's begin there. May tends to have less rain than June or July, the wildflowers are in full bloom, and Nature seems to be coming alive after winter deep sleep. Prices are lower, and cruise ships less crowded than they will be once school's out in a few weeks. And *bears-!* Alaskan black and brown bears wake up in early May (grizzlies a little later) and are they hungry! Since salmon are not yet running in the inland streams, bears tend to be active, hunting food along shorelines, often visible from the ship or near streams in ports.

June (especially earlier in the month) is a sweet spot before crowds descend upon Alaska's wonders, but it's considered peak season, so bargains are rare. Moose give birth around June, so you might be able to glimpse a calf, if you're lucky. Bears, otters, minks, orca, whales, and other creatures have babies, too, so keep an eye out. June has the longest days all year, with summer solstice falling mid-month. Now's your chance to soak up twenty-two-hour days. If you're not a fan of darkness, like me, you'll love being about to read without a light on deck nearly all night long.

Wildlife is visibly abundant, with whales making their journey back into Alaskan waters from Hawaii in May and June. If you know what to look for, you'll spot some of the many humpback whales feeding with their young. Baby whales are playful, and they sure behave better than their human counterparts. Often, at first glance, it's hard to tell where Mommy Whale leaves off and Baby begins; they're that close. Have you ever tried to get a toddler to stay beside you?

Baby bald eagles are old enough to leave the nest, called aeries, this month. If you're lucky, you may get to witness a fledgling's first flight lessons. Did you know American Bald Eagles don't get their characteristic white heads and tail feathers until their fifth summer? Before that, they're eagle-shaped, but a mottled grey-brown color.

July is the pivot point, the absolute middle of the Alaska cruise season, and there are advantages. More cruises are booked for July than any other month, and all but a very few sail at full capacity. If you're determined to go to Alaska in July, book far in advance to get a good price. Rain often blows through Southeast Alaska this time of year. Bring a waterproofed, warm jacket; more about packing later.

Alaska has a short growing season, but very long daylight hours, making for enormous produce. July is when fresh local fruits and vegetables hit the markets, and your plate, if you eat in town. Tidewater glaciers are on the move in the warmer months, so your chances of seeing calving increase.

August is alive in Southeast Alaska. It's still summer, but if you look around, you'll see signs of nature gearing up for winter, at least in small ways. Salmon fill the streams, and bears line the banks of the same streams; one on a desperate race to get home, the other on a quest to pack on fat against winter's cold. Bald eagles can also be seen congregating near salmon-spawning streams. Although cruise prices remain high, August is ideal for visiting Alaska. Weather is still warm, the days are long, and all of the whales and migratory birds have yet to head south for the winter.

September in Southeast Alaska is when autumn starts to sink in. Although the weather is often still mild, there's a feeling of awareness of the inevitable winter ahead. Once the kids are in school, the towns quiet down. Wildlife is stocking up for the winter, putting on fat layers and thicker winter fur. Some have already begun their long migration to points south, but there are still plenty to see. Black and brown bears are busy stuffing themselves in preparation for winter hibernation. Early snowfalls grace higher peaks like powdered sugar, and mountainsides morph into beautiful flame-colored shades of gold and yellow as the leaves turn colors in September. Prices on cruises tend to be a few hundred dollars lower, but of course that also depends on capacity. With increasing days of rain and winds, there's a good chance one of your excursions could get rained out. Especially ones involving a helicopter or small plane; pilots are picky about crashing in high winds, and flying through weather that looks a lot like a car wash simply isn't safe.

Yes, any part of Alaska's cruise season is awesome!

Just Go. That's my advice. But you may want to take into account some factors in your planning, including which dates fit your personal schedule, price, and specific itineraries. Figure out what is most important to see and do in Alaska, and plan your cruise around the top items on your list. Most everything is available through the whole cruise season, but there are pros and cons to consider.

Is one time better than another to book your cruise? Mid-June through mid-July has the most daylight, the longest days, which can make your vacation feel much longer. But you stand a better chance of seeing the elusive Northern Lights later in the year, when the night sky actually gets dark. Most ships' captains turn off the upper deck lights so you can relish the deep night sky.

During spring, wildflowers bloom along the Inside Passage, and you're more likely to see larger animals migrating. Gray whales finally finish their trip from Hawaii in early June. June's also a prime time to see orcas, Minke whales and Pacific white-sided dolphins near the shoreline. Late springtime is when the glaciers are most active, calving house-sized bergs into the sea with waves high enough to surf on...don't even consider it. It's already been done, and that documentary was scary!

May generally brings less rain or snow and more sunshine in Southeast Alaska than other months. With winter's icy grip in the rearview mirror, temperatures rise in May and daylight is lengthy, making for long, pleasant days. The first Alaskan wildflowers begin blooming for the summer, and migratory birds arrive, flocking to bodies of water to settle in for a summer's feast. With 18 to 22 hours of daylight (more than your home, I'm guessing), there's plenty of opportunity for exploring, whether you spend your time hanging over a ship's rail, paddling a kayak, hiking a less traveled trail, or lounging on a balcony watching Alaska glide by. With most kids still in school, ships tend to have a slightly more mature passenger list. I love children, but I can't deny this can make for a more peaceful onboard experience.

In May and early June, cruise prices are often lower, usually by several hundred dollars per person over the same trip a month later. I've paid under $90 per day on several trips to Alaska; cheaper than a Holiday Inn, and the scenery is better, too. Shore excursions are often about twenty percent cheaper in the first part of the cruise season. With fewer families booking cruises before the kids are out for summer, you'll find a wider selection of onboard cabins, especially adjoining ones. Same number of ships, though, as every cruise line is eager to get a jump on the Alaska season!

Spotting wildlife is always unpredictable in Alaska, but your best bet of coming upon wildlife ashore is probably late May and early June, when mothers and their new babies tend to be out and about near shorelines. They spend mid-summers a little further inland. Note: prime bear-watching season is not until late June or early July, so don't waste your money booking a bear-seeking excursion in May. They hibernate all winter, and can be a little lazy about waking up come springtime.

Now, one form of wildlife is tough to avoid. Alaska's state bird, alias the mosquito, is legendary. I think they have a bad attitude. The little beggars seem more aggressive in Alaska, and fearless. They're big, the size of mini cupcakes, and they *hurt*! I swear they can bite clear to the bone marrow. After the end of May, just plan on mosquitoes being part of the scenery, often in cloud-form, especially away from the main streets of towns. Early and late in the season will have fewer mosquitoes. They don't hatch until mid-June, and they've died off by September. But *in between*-! Don't let them stop you, but feel free to fight back by wearing insect repellant daily. Even people who typically don't get bitten seem to taste better to Alaskan mosquitoes.

If you're planning to tack on a land tour to Denali, don't book a cruise in May. The park doesn't open up until early June. Even then, plan on unpredictable weather any week of the season. You may have 70 degrees at bedtime and wake up to six inches of fresh snow before breakfast. The Great Mountain doesn't plan around tourists.

Fishing is good during any month; there are just different species of salmon that peak as the weeks go by. You'll want to avoid salmon fishing in August and September, unless it's the deep-sea variety. Late in the summer, salmon return upstream to spawn. It's a seriously tough journey, and by the time they reach the streams they're pretty well spent, beat up, battered, and not good eating. Deep-sea fishing excursions are great all summer. They'll even pack and ship anything you catch, delivered to your doorstep once you arrive home week, frozen solid, ideal for dinner and bragging about the one that got away. I'll talk about seafood later on.

Summer berry-picking on shore is best late in August or early September. Those wild strawberries are so sweet, they're even good green! Salmon berries, huckleberries, blackberries, thimbleberries, wild blueberries, apricot-scented cloudberries, lingonberries... all free for the munching as you explore Alaska's wilderness. I advise reading a field guide before you go if you plan to snack while hiking. Alaska has several poisonous wild berry varieties, including the well-named baneberry, which can stop a person's heart after eating less than a handful. That's no way to wrap up a vacation.

If you want to see fall foliage ashore, wait until the first week of September or later. If you're planning on fall colors being the highlight of your trip, you're in the wrong part of the continent...cruises in New England and the Canadian Maritimes stand a far better chance of overwhelming your senses with leaf-colors.

I'll talk more about weather later, but don't let that hamper your plans. I live near Seattle, where rainy, drizzly, gloomy, dark days far outnumber sunny ones. I decided long ago that if I let the weather influence my plans, I'd never get outdoors at all. Just pack layers, and be ready for anything. Generally, Southeast Alaska's best weather is between mid-June and mid-August. That varies, of course: you could wake to ice on your balcony in July, or get a good sunburn in late September. Depending on your plan for the day, you could do both in the same afternoon!

Which Cruise Line Is Right For You?

Great, you've made up your mind to cruise to Alaska! Now, how do you choose the best cruise line for your needs? Truth be told, the mainstream cruise lines are more similar than you might think. All vie for your business, and all try to provide an experience so wonderful, you'll want to come back, with friends in tow. They do have their own vibe, so to speak, and we'll look at each line's strengths.

For me, itinerary weighs heavily in my decision-making process. Some cruise lines spend much more time in ports than others, and with so much to see in Alaska, that makes a big difference. Some ships are in port only a half day, not allowing enough time for a lengthy tour or exploring further afield. Some towns are small enough that you can see much of the place in a few hours. A short stop there may be fine. Pay attention to the itinerary even more than the ship. It's Alaska, after all, and you don't want to miss out!

Along with some smaller cruise lines, the main lines sailing to Alaska are: Princess, Holland America, Carnival, Norwegian, Royal Caribbean, Disney, Celebrity, Oceania, Regent Seven Seas, Seaborne, Crystal, and Silversea. The first five tend to be mainstream, while Oceania, Regent Seven Seas, Seaborne, Crystal, and Silversea are most upscale, and most expensive. Each has its own flavor, but if the opportunity arises, go to Alaska!

Let's look at each cruise line's strengths.

Carnival tends toward non-stop onboard activity; it's not a staid atmosphere by anybody's imagination. Waterslides, outdoor movie screens, and group games keeps the party atmosphere hopping. The mega ships even have parades. The kids' program, Camp Carnival, is divided into five age groups, with age-appropriate activities for each. Arts and crafts, wading pools, arcade games, computers and even candy-making machines keep kids happy while parents play in the casino or disco. Some passengers might find the frequent announcements for yet more fun a bit overwhelming.

Celebrity Cruise Line

Celebrity tends to have a more grown-up atmosphere than Carnival. It's known to attract "foodies" with its trendy menus, but you'll find plenty of comfort foods as well. Catering to active cruisers, Celebrity prides itself on modern luxury, with none of the old-world stuffiness and all of its classiness. It's not just for adults, though; their ships offer supervised activities for three age groups, plus a teen center onboard every ship.

Disney Cruise Line

No surprise, **Disney** excels in entertainment, with production shows that bring the Disney experience to life. Dining onboard is on a rotating basis, unless you opt for the adult-only specialty restaurant. By the end of the cruise, each passenger will dine in every venue onboard on a set schedule, each with its own flair. Disney has kids covered, with activities catering to those as young as three months. Parades, character meet-and-greets, meals with the princesses, and a boundlessly enthusiastic crew makes Disney a great choice for families. Don't count on any bargain-basement prices; Disney can easily cost a third more than another cruise line on the same itinerary.

Holland America

HAL has come a long way from its formal, geriatric persona, although these are still the only ships on which I've seen jigsaw puzzles laid out in the library! Catering to passengers who love to learn and soak up any new experience, HAL is also known for service. Entertainment has improved dramatically in the last few years, with live music and blues clubs onboard, even dueling pianos on some ships. A naturalist-lecturer and locations specialist is onboard every ship to let you know what you're seeing and what not to miss. Holland America has partnered with Microsoft to offer onboard classes, including how to use online free programs to showcase your gorgeous Alaska videos and photographs. HAL's children's program promotes education as well, including galley tours and cooking classes for ages three and up.

Norwegian Cruise Line

NCL pioneered the "freestyle" cruising policy—eat when, where, and with whom you want—and just about every other cruise line has copied some version of it. NCL's ships are easy to spot; some call their bright artwork garish, but it's certainly not stuffy. Plan on dance parties every night, Vegas-style entertainment, and plenty of chances to socialize with other passengers. Family-friendly NCL offers sports competitions, movies, demos, even a bowling alley on some ships. (At last, a valid-sounding excuse for that bad score: The Ship Was Moving. Of course, that's more believable once the ship is out of port.) The supervised Kid's Crew program covers three age groups, with games, storytelling, arts and crafts, pajama parties, pirate themed-treasure hunts and free-play time, while a designated teen space includes DJ lessons, nightly parties, movies and arcade games.

Princess

I love Princess' service and attention to detail. I'm still not sure how just about every uniformed staff member manages to greet passengers by name...and they'll have another batch next week! Ship activities tend to be low-key but with an interesting variety. Princess ships focus on educational programs, including wildlife and the environment, and it spills into the kids' programs as well. The first to provide walkie-talkie type radios for parents to keep tabs on independent-but-young kids onboard, Princess caters to families as well as adults. Onboard shows are often Broadway quality, although shorter.

Royal Caribbean

RCCL is a standout with regards to multi-generational cruising, and Alaska is an ideal place to bring the whole gang. Besides the wonders of Alaska itself, there's plenty to do onboard. Depending on the class of ship you choose, there's ice skating, a surf simulator, mini golf, water slides, and rock climbing, and an emphasis on onboard recreation that spills into shore excursions. Although Royal does the "fancy" aspect of cruising beautifully, as you'd expect, the program for children is surprisingly good. Supervised activities for ages three through seventeen are onboard every ship, as well as guided parent-and-child baby and toddler sessions daily. Entertainment on Royal is engaging for all ages, from review bands to disco.

Crystal Cruise Line

Crystal is all-inclusive luxury at a pace designed for discerning travelers, and typically attracts a more mature crowd. Not specifically catering to young families, some sailings don't offer any activities for children; it depends on how many kids will be onboard that trip. Shipboard activities tend to be education-oriented: you can learn to program your camera and attend a lecture on the history of the Tlingit, but there are no belly-flop contests on the pool deck. Service is top-notch, with a very low crew-to-passenger ratio and more space per traveler onboard. Seeking some pampering? Crystal awaits, but plan on paying for it.

Oceania

Oceania is known for flat-out luxury with an emphasis on cultural enrichment, local foods and upscale dining, superior service and well-stocked libraries. Ships tend to be small, under seven hundred passengers, making hands-on activities easier with a more intimate experience overall. Plan on more lectures than nightlife and a pretty sophisticated passenger list.

Regent Seven Seas

Regent Seven Seas is elegance at sea; no other way to describe it. Even without official formal nights, the atmosphere can be a little too stuffy for some folks, but the service is amazing. I'm not sure if they train staff and crew in mind reading, but they do seem to be able to anticipate passengers' wishes before the person finished wishing it. There are plenty of onboard lectures and local experts, offering a good enrichment aspect in Alaska.

Silversea

Practically dripping with luxury, **Silversea** focuses on relaxation combined with cultural enrichment, and the fine dining rivals any land restaurant. While the dress code can be restrictive for some, the sense of escapism can't be beat. Silversea unabashedly caters to a mature traveler, with no activities for kids and not much in the way of nightlife. Most staterooms have private balconies.

What kind of cabin is best in Alaska?

It's totally up to you! You may want a luxurious suite with a private balcony to enjoy breakfast as you sail into another of Alaska's ports. You may instead opt to economize with an inside cabin so you can have more money to spend on experiences, considering a stateroom just a place to sleep. *Cruise Tips From the Cruise Addict's Wife* and *More Cruise Tips From the Cruise Addict's Wife* both detail how to select a cabin in more detail than here. Whatever category of cabin you choose, remember, every passenger on any ship has access to the same dining room, same shows, onboard activities, same tours and the same gorgeous scenery. It's up to you! There's an excerpt from my book on choosing a cabin at the end of this book, so read on!

You may want a balcony to sprawl on, watching for whales as the scenery goes by, or you may decide it's not for you. In Glacier Bay or the other big tidewater glaciers, it's best to be up on deck for a 360-degree view anyway. A balcony can be chilly, and we had a stateroom where the balcony door banged in the cold wind all night, until I finally got up and wedged a folded paper in the track. Those ubiquitous onboard sale ads do come in handy.

On the other hand, one of my nicest memories is, after the ship pulled away from the glacier's face, sitting on my balcony watching icebergs, and bergies float leisurely past, not a care in the world. My cell phone didn't even get reception in Glacier Bay, and I do love silence. Best two hours I've spent recently.

Which side of the ship is best for viewing glaciers?

POSH means "port out, starboard home," but in Alaska, scenery is all around and pretty much non-stop. If you book an Inside Passage cruise, you can see land on both sides of the ship a good portion of the trip. If you opt for a cross-Gulf sailing, you're likely to spot whales and small boats in any direction. When the ship slips up the narrow fjords to the tidewater glaciers, the viewing will be equally good from both sides of the ship. On every ship, captains make a slow 360-degree turn back into open water, so you'll see whatever side you missed on the way in.

What is there to do in Alaska?

Oh, my goodness—I've never met a bored cruise passenger in Alaska! Most are bubbling over with stories about their day and plans for tomorrow. I did, however, meet a couple on a cruise who somehow failed to read the cruise information...let me tell you the story.

After two days at sea, the ship spent ten hours in Ketchikan. That evening, as the ship sailed out of port, Husband and I relaxed in a lounge with a few other couples, new friends we'd just met. Talk turned to "What did you do today?"

One couple had attended the Great Alaskan Lumberjack Show and explored the Southeast Alaska Discovery Center. Another spent the morning at Saxman Village and bought cute Alaska-themed toys for the grandchildren at home. We'd shopped on Creek Street, visited the museum, rode the funicular to Cape Fox and then hiked to the Totem Heritage Center before feasting on crab cakes and locally made sodas.

I noticed the last couple sat silent, intent on whoever was speaking.

At last the man blurted, "You mean we can *get off the ship?!"*

My jaw dropped. How had he managed to overlook hundreds of people streaming down the gangway and the goings-on on the pier all day?

Whatever you plan to do in Alaska, don't be those people. Read everything you can lay your hands on about your cruise, the ship, the ports, all of it! Or you could travel with someone like me, a compulsive reader. My friends call me Information Booth. I'm not sure it's a compliment, but I am skilled at trip-planning!

As I detail in my other cruise books, you want to be the most informed passenger on any cruise ship. How awful would it be to come home and learn you'd missed something wonderful, *right there*, simply because you didn't know it existed? The younger generation calls it FOMO, a fear of missing out. Generally, that's just silly, but on a cruise...go for it, you may never get back here again!

Oh, the other couple? I saw them the next morning, first in line to disembark.

In Alaska, as in most ports worldwide, you can stay onboard, get off and wander, book a formal ship-sponsored shore excursions, take your chances with the ubiquitous guy-with-a-sign jaunt or ask a local what they recommend, stay close to the ship where touristy shops abound, pick up a walking tour map from a visitor's center, or simple head off on a nice quiet walk on your own, perhaps in a quest for local foods or artwork. It's up to you. Make the most of your cruise!

Do a little research at home, and plan what you most wish to do and see, or you'll end up like Tom's family.

My family was in Juneau, and we had a plan. Throughout the morning, we noticed a family silently tailing us a few paces back. When we walked, they'd walk, when we stopped, they stopped, when we looked back, they glanced away in a vain attempt to become invisible.

As they wrangled a table next to ours at a lunch spot, the man finally admitted, "You seem to know where to go and what to do, and we don't have a clue. Hi, I'm Tom, and this is my family." Once proper introductions were out of the way, we spent a pleasant afternoon together.

Do a little research before you leave home. I suggest an internet search for "things to do in (name of port)" in each port your cruise visits. Next, do a similar search for "inexpensive things to do in (name of port)". Expand it to "free things to do it (name of port)" and you'll be amazed. Hiking trails, totem site, visitors centers and local museums, craft groups, artist walks, free walking tour maps are just a few of the opportunities available for the looking! Alaska has so much to offer!

Ship-sponsored shore excursions in Alaska can be very pricey, some of the highest in the world of cruising. Go ahead, if it's important to you; this may be once in a lifetime for you. Or not...how many times have I returned to Alaska? While the price ranges might be unlike other shore tours you've encountered before, the experiences are even more incredible. Anything involving flight doesn't come cheaply, but Alaska is one of the best places to grab an aerial view -- especially as planes are a regular mode of transportation in a state where many locales aren't accessible by road. Floatplanes to bear-viewing parks or helicopters to sled dog camps or tundra high above sea level leave an indelible cruise memory. However, bear in mind a four-hour flight costs roughly the same as a flight to Europe.

I have a fear of Missing Something Wonderful. That's why I read up on any place we visit. I'm eager to see and do as much as possible in the time I'm *anywhere new,* figuring I may never get back there again. The Cruise Addict and I like to book private tours in most ports. I calculate we save 45%- 65% over a ship-sponsored tour, and we see much more, while having the flexibility to do exactly what we want. Plus, I'm not a fan of crowds. Most ships' tours are on buses, which is like packing your very own mob with you, all day.

Forget the cattle calls and packed motor coach (really, just a bus) tours; savvy cruisers know that hiring a private tour guide is often the best way to visit a port of call. The cruise lines don't like to hear it (a huge profit on cruises comes from shore excursions) but the advantages of going it on your own are numerous. You can set a personalized itinerary, travel alone or in a smaller group, and see only what you want to see, and at your own pace. While you could get carried away and spend a fortune, we've always saved significant money going on our own.

The cruise lines push hard for their shore excursions; that's a major money -maker for them, along with drink sales and bingo. Ship-sponsored shore tours not all bad.

They're okay if you're a fearful traveler who likes being herded in a nice, safe group rather than seeing and doing more on your own in an unfamiliar place. Personally, the only times I've found them useful is as an airport transfer in the destination city. It's nice to see something new on the way to the airport, without having to wrangle your luggage. The one in Galveston that stopped at the Houston Space Center was especially fun. Overall, I prefer going off on my own, or with a one-car-sized tour, free to go as I choose or redirect on a whim.

Having done your research at home, you may well find you don't need a tour at all. Don't bother with a live tour guide when main attractions are easily accessible. You can skip a tour if you know where you're going, such as Fort Adams in Newport, RI, or The Freedom Trail in Boston. You surely don't need a tour to find the Point Roberts tram in Juneau; it's visible from the ship! A paid walking tour to the shops is silly.

 If you do choose a ship-sponsored tour, read the fine print and know what you're paying for. For example, cruise lines offer tours to the Great Alaskan Lumberjack Show in Ketchikan. A guide will meet you (and

40+ other people) and walk you the two blocks to the show's venue, where you will pick a seat anywhere you choose. At the end, you're on your own. Cost: $49 or more. Alternatively, you could walk the two blocks to the show venue, buy a ticket, and pick a seat anywhere you choose. Tickets cost $37, less for kids. Is it worth an extra $12 per person to follow a guide two blocks on foot, when you can see the place from the gangway?

To save even more money, before you leave home, do an online search for discount tickets to places you plan on seeing. Groupon, etc, can save a good percentage off entry fees , and all you have to do is print a ticket at home.

You can often find museums, restaurants, parks, and incredible sites you had no idea existed within walking distance or an easy cab ride away. Most ports have a Tourism Center right by the pier. It's a good first stop. Pick up a free map and brochure, and you're on your way.

In your planning, I suggest seeking out cheap and free things to do in any port. I like visitors' centers; they're a microcosm of local lore and history, neatly condensed. Local parks are often fun, as are quirky little shops. Window shopping costs nothing, contrary to Husband's claims. While you're browsing, ask the clerk what they recommend you see next. Best fudge on the planet, free gold panning, a local fossil field open to the public? What are you waiting for?

Most ports in Alaska are walkable, if all you want to do is explore on your own. Renting a car is not really wise, since so few towns are connected, but hiring a cab to show you nearby places too far to walk to is a good idea. In Skagway, for example, you may want to see Dyea, what's left of it, but hiking to the old gosh-rush-town-turned-ghost-town would eat up most of your time in port. Even if you rented a car to head up into the Yukon Territory, your rental car agency will likely warn you to avoid Dyea, due to the...well, they call it a road, but that gully-washed track of potholed gravel isn't good for rental cars. Better to catch a ride with a 4x4 type taxi driver who knows where the worst pits are located.

In most cruise ports, I recommend going off on your own, once you've researched what not to miss. I even suggest renting a car in many ports...but not Alaska. It's not a drivable state, and a car isn't practical. Only 20% of Alaska's roads are paved, versus an average 91% for the other 49 states. The road in Juneau, the capital, is only forty-four miles end to end, and a lot of that is gravel. There's even less pavement in other towns!

The exception is Skagway, where renting a car is a great idea. Driving up into the Yukon and British Columbia is a gorgeous day trip! You can easily download mile-by mile guides that will make your adventure unforgettable online. We stopped at abandoned silver mines, lakes and rivers, a beaver lodge, and the wildlife was amazing. I saw a few bears, porcupines, beavers, and a coyote so big and fluffy, I thought at first it was something else entirely. They're rather scrawny at home. The coyote lunged and ate a furry creature in one gulp, so fast I think its heart was still beating when it hit the coyote's stomach. Yuck, but fascinating!

The best part of that day was the silence. We passed seven overstuffed buses first thing in the morning, and saw more at the iconic *Welcome to the Yukon* sign a while later. Other than that, I think we saw under a handful of vehicles the whole day.

Emerald Lake is a gemstone-colored lake in the middle of nowhere. It gets its gorgeous color from the microscopic diatoms, the very same ones that give the Caribbean water its lovely colors. How did that happen? If you go, don't miss the bakery halfway to Carcross. The sign says "Eat Here Or We'll Both Starve," and the luscious homemade cinnamon rolls are the size of a fedora.

Private Tours

A good way to see what's available is to read over the shore excursions offered by cruise lines in each port. If deep-sea fishing, a salmon bake, whale watching, or gold panning catches your eye, make note. Book small tours directly through the tour company's web page or ask your travel agent to arrange a private tour. Reserve them well before you set sail; good ones fill up fast.

To plot your day, whether it's a small tour or on your own, try http://www.tomsportguides.com/, tripadvisor.com, or do an online search for each port's name, and "tourism." I've had great luck by simply googling "shore excursion Skagway" or whatever port you're looking at. Typing "tour," or "day tour" also works, but specifying "shore excursion" narrows the field to companies accustomed to working with cruise passengers' time constraints. It also eliminates the awkward need to make your way to the pick-up point, often at a hotel somewhere. Tours labeled "shore excursion' automatically pick up and drop off right at the port", often right near the bottom of the gangway.

A tour you arrange yourself has so many advantages! Do some research and find private guides so that you can do exactly what you want to do. If you're in a private car and wish to stop at that waterfall over there, speak up. You can't do that on a tour bus. Your driver might even offer you a paper cup to taste the icy water. Alaska is the only US state where giardia doesn't exist. Even without the beaver-fever bacteria risk, I'm still leery of outdoor water... I just don't know if some wandering creature pooped upstream, and I'm not chancing getting sick.

It's easier than you think! Last year, I arranged ten tours in ten ports in five countries, back to back, from my own computer. I had to factor in time zones, but email was easy—I never even made a phone call. Each was an incredible experience. Alaska's even easier. Tours in Alaska are pricey, but you can save quite a bit by booking them yourself.

Once you've narrowed your search down to several potential tour guides, start sending emails. In your initial contact, you'll want to state the date that you'll be in port, how many people are in your party and tell them what kind of tour you are looking for. For example, "It's our first time in Juneau, we want to see as much as we can, we're not interested in a dog sled kennel but would enjoy glacier caving, there are five of us ranging in age from teen to retired, and we'll be on the Gemini Angel on September 7th."

Tour companies often have set tours, which you can customize, within reason. If you really want to see La Brea Tar Pits, the confluence of the Columbia River, or the cemetery where the Titanic victims lie, speak up ahead of time. Well, modify that list for Alaska.

And don't worry about missing the ship. Tour companies deal with cruise passengers all the time, and they know getting you back on time is critical to their livelihood. You have the power to write a review online, and they know their future business depends on you writing a positive one!

Traditional/Local Foods

I believe part of traveling, the be-where-you-are part, includes seeking out local foods. Brunswick Stew in Savannah, conch chowder in Key West, lobster in Boston, loco moco in Hawaii, steak in Omaha, catfish and hush puppies in Georgia; for me, it's a big part of the experience! Alaska's no different.

Wild Alaska seafood can be found in almost every restaurant, from mouth-watering fish and chips to heaping fisherman's platters with an array of...well, pretty much all of it. The most memorable and expensive meal I've ever eaten included a spread of Alaska's seafood delicacies, topped with a king crab leg so big, it overflowed the platter. Tucked in the corner was a lonely spring of broccoli, a nod to nutrition. Good thing I believe in sharing.

With its long coastline and wide ocean, Alaska's known for seafood. Crab and salmon, of course, are king in Alaska. Five types of wild salmon abound, plus milder white fish including black cod/sablefish, pollock, sole, flounder and halibut, along with scallops, oysters, spotted shrimp, and it's all delicious. Alaska's seafood is wonderful! Well, I can't recommend sea cucumbers. They're basically a large water-filled slug, often served pickled. None for me, thanks!

Hungry for some Alaskan crab? King crab is the best-known (and priciest), but many people favor Dungeness' sweeter taste. A local woman confided, "I like Dungeness crab better than King. It's not as rich, so I can eat a lot more of it." Is that your goal? Smaller varieties are every bit as delicious, including snow crab, which you'll find in many restaurants' crab cakes.

Planning to take the flavors of Alaska home? Salmon canneries line the coast, with more on boats out at sea. Canned salmon, dried salmon, salmon jerky, salmon spread and jam, smoked salmon in many varieties, fresh salmon with promised shipping to your doorstep; salmon is just about everywhere. I've even seen salmon soda, although I can't say I recommend it. You have to a draw a line somewhere.

Not a seafood fan? With the very long summer days, produce grows sweet and enormous. Alaska is known for wild berries, served in pies, cobblers, crumbles, crisps, etc, in just about every local restaurant during summer months. Mild, tangy spruce-tip jams and wild-berry jams and syrups are available in many shops for taking home.

If you're interested in sampling more exotic local fare, get your taste buds ready for Alaska! Wild game abounds, and local chefs make hay with the land's bounty. Start with elk or venison, or move on to wild boar in delicious ham sandwiches, reindeer-caribou sausage, jerky, and pepperoni, bear steaks, buffalo steaks and burgers or rich lamb. I highly recommend you splurge on at least one land-based meal in Alaska!

Onboard, most cruise ships serve a version of Baked Alaska, a nod to a 1960s dessert made of ice cream, cake or pie crust, topped with a heap of meringue, torched to brown the tips. It's far from authentic, but tasty. One cruise line that really ought to remain nameless serves a dish called Alaska Glacier Meatloaf. It's hard to describe; as if a badly seasoned meatloaf ran through a blender on its way to a salt factory, topped with overcooked, gummy mashed potato "glacier" and peas the color of a dead leprechaun. If you see it on a menu, I'd suggest steering clear.

Glaciers—it's Alaska, after all!

Mashed potatoes aside, glaciers are incredible. I met a person who griped, "Glacier, schmaysher, a whole lot of dirty old ice. You can't even see through it." My jaw dropped. Clearly, she didn't know what she was looking at!

That crystalline ice is hundreds of years old; it may have been a mere snowstorm during the Crusades or when Plato kicked up gravel with his fancy sandals. Glacier's deep gemstone-blue hue is caused by decades of pressure, squeezing snowflakes so tightly together, their reflective surfaces no longer reflect light at all. The bluest ice is the oldest, while the whiter ice is less compressed. That so-called dirt is the churned-up tracks of two or more glaciers ramming together somewhere far uphill, roiling on top of one another, picking up rocks and debris as the glacier made its way to the sea over several centuries, while the rest of the world went about its business. This just isn't any old ice!

Impressed by the sheer size of a glacier? Bering Glacier in Alaska measures about one-hundred-eighteen *miles* long. Margerie Glacier's face rises 350 feet off the ocean's surface, with at least a couple hundred feet more below the waterline. Look at an iceberg floating by; easy to do from the deck of a ship. Yes, you can see the part above the water, but look closer. It's said that ninety percent of icebergs are under the water's surface. Tidewater glaciers are significantly bigger than the part you can see, and that part is plenty awe-inspiring. Some ice bergs are small, called bergies or bergie bits, but others can be as high as a three-story building. They provide a relatively safe rest stop for seals and sea lions, away from the ever-hungry orcas.

The biggest glacier visited by cruise ships, Hubbard, is beyond impressive. With a face six miles wide and forty stories high, it's incredible, and you can only get close to it in a cruise ship. On good days, you'll get to within a half mile of the face, but on days of very active calving, ships have to keep their distance for safety.

Did you know the Native American and First Nations people believe glaciers are alive? Scoff if you wish, but standing near a groaning, creaking, hissing glacier, with the occasional crack like a cannon shot, it's easy to feel their spirit as they move down the valley. Of course, they're alive.

If your bucket list calls for a seeing a real live glacier, or better yet, an actively calving one, then you should pick a cruise ship that goes to the one you want to see. The glaciers in College Fjord and Hubbard Glacier are on many itineraries, due to their relatively easy-to-get-to locations. Ships can show them off to passengers without a major expenditure of fuel and time.

On a cruise ship of, say, 2000 passengers, you may only see a couple hundred, except for embarkation day. And Glacier Watching Day. On any cruise ship, rails will be lined with passengers, eager to lay eyes on glacial ice. I'm not sure where they hide out other times.

Hubbard Glacier is one of the few glaciers in the world that's actually expanding. On a clear day, you can see the massive sheet of ice stretching up the valley, and calving is frequent. I saw an apartment building-sized ice berg crumble before my eyes and fall into the ocean. I actually felt my heart stop, just from the glory of that!

The weather is not always cooperative in the fjords however and fog can be an enemy any day of the cruise season. I've managed to luck out, by crossing finger and other applicable body parts. I met a sad couple from New Zealand who'd been disappointed by heavy fog on their day in Yucatat Bay, unable to catch even a glimpse of the glacier. Seems to me the Universe could have cooperated for a couple on a once-in-a-lifetime cruise twelve thousand miles from home, but it didn't.

Glacier Bay is amazing; there's no other word for it. Several cruise lines go there, but access is very limited. Double check your itinerary if it matters to you. Glacier Bay is a designated Unesco Biosphere. To preserve that, only two cruise ships per day are permitted, and that's only for ninety-two days out of a year.

Glaciers don't perform on demand. You may luck out, as I have many times, and have a clear, 55-degree day with house-sized icebergs crashing into the seas every few minutes. Another trip, sleet fell, the sideways variety. The weather was so foul, it wasn't worth the words to tell you about it. The next time I was there, people complained of sunburn. You'll see people in parkas, and others in shorts, no matter what time of year you go.

On a couple of trips, the glacier was so active, a thick ice floe made of broken bergies made traversing the fjord too dangerous, and the ship's captain gave up not far into the channel. One of our friends said when he was there, a massive chunk of ice right calved off, raced across the channel, and a wave washed up and over the open promenade deck, soaking passengers who couldn't get out of the way fast enough. Such instances are rare, but I'm envious. When early Russian, then European, explorers ventured into Glacier Bay in the 1700s, they counted a total of one glacier. In the years since then, that glacier has retreated more than sixty-five miles, exposing twenty separate glaciers.

Tracy Arm is a breathtakingly beautiful, but cold, journey up a long fjord to North and South Sawyer Glaciers. Chilly air is trapped between the high sides of the fjord, and pours over the ships the way opening your freezer on a hot summer day feels, on a larger scale. Sawyer glacier splits midway up into two sections. When the glacier is actively calving, it's really active. Icebergs choke the narrow passage and can prevent the cruise ships from actually getting to the glacier.

In my trips up Tracy Arm, I've only seen the glacier about half the time...and a few of those times, I almost wish we'd turned back sooner! On one cruise, our intrepid captain sped up as the ice in the water thickened. We could plainly hear ice chunks clanking against the hull, some the size of my living room. I don't know what was worse, potentially missing seeing the glacier or thinking the ship could be taking on water at any minute. A cruise ship hull is surprisingly thin, a fact that captain seemed to disregard. Whew!

If your particular cruise doesn't visit Glacier Bay, you could consider taking a tour from a nearby port. Sometimes smaller boats can maneuver better than cruise ships.

Weather

Yes, Alaska is cold; everybody knows that, right? Back up a bit. Unless you're heading above the Arctic Circle, it's not as cold as you might think, at least during the summer. And even when it's pretty chilly by Lower Forty-eight standards, it's common to see children playing, wearing tee shirts and shorts, same as kids do in Iowa in July.

I suspect it's like Seattle. Some local residents freely admit they lie outright, saying it rains every day of the year, mainly to discourage more tourists in an already-overcrowded area. And really, it only rains about ten months of the year in northwest Washington...and drips of the trees the rest of the time. When we moved to western Washington, we simply decided to enjoy and go and do; if you wait for decent weather here, you can wait for months.

We pretty much have two seasons here: Rainy Season and Tourist Season. Some years, summer is canceled, outright. There was that year a few years back, when home had exactly six days over 70 degrees all year...sadly, the very week we were on an Alaskan cruise. Yes, I completely missed all the summer weather that year. Sigh.

I had a friend who lived in southern California. She moaned, "Oh, yuck, another sunny day with clear blue skies, not even a piddly little cloud for variety. Sunshine, hot, dry days, that's all we ever get!" I couldn't relate, not one bit.

Southeast Alaska, where most of the cruise ships ply the waters, is partially a rain forest. The area around Ketchikan measures rainfall in feet, not inches, and the moss on the trees is truly impressive, inches thick! Bring a waterproof jacket and a good attitude, and get out there—you're going to love Alaska!

Alaskan weather is defined by its unpredictability. It's always unreliable; it just is. They say if you're not happy with the weather, just wait a while, it'll change. Even if you check the long-range forecast before you leave home, plan on it being wrong at least part of every day. No monotony here!

Alaska's big, really big, and the weather varies by the time of year and how far north you go, same as every other place on the planet. The far north regions, near the Arctic Circle, are downright frigid a good part of the year, but cruise ships don't venture that far north. Southeast Alaska, where cruises do go, can be chilly and balmy, often in the same week. I've noticed sunny days turning suddenly brisk and rainy, and—and vice versa. Alaska's weather swings wildly, with temperatures jumping or falling thirty degrees, often in a matter of hours.

The key is to simply be prepared for all types of weather on your Alaskan cruise. In other words, bring sunscreen, gloves, and plan on wearing thin layers you can jettison or add throughout the day. Sadly, this means you likely can't get by with just a carry-on for your cruise...it's tough to pack light when you need warm clothing! More on what to pack later.

Cruise ships move around the planet all year long, seeking the best weather, and the best time of year for each locale. In the Maritimes, ships seeking "the colors" of autumn leaves don't go in the springtime, when there are no leaves to see. With only one exception, you can't book a cruise to the northern reaches of Scandinavia during the winter, but South America is lovely during their summer months. It's the same with Alaska. When the winter winds blow across the rippling tundra and the sun rises above the horizon just enough to set again, residents hunker down in their quiet towns, and both animals and humans think of hibernating.

The cruise season in Alaska hits the best months, mid-April to mid-October, weather-wise. If you take a cruise ship, you may see a bare dusting of snow, but you're not going to freeze solid. In fact, a few times when I've been on a cruise to Alaska, shorts and tees were more common than parkas, and I had a memorable sunburn in Juneau.

Make up your mind to be prepared for whatever weather Alaska throws at you, and you'll be fine. Clouds and rain might roll in, the sun may make you wish you had more layers to modestly remove, the temperature may swing 40 degrees while you're having lunch--welcome to Alaska!

And of course, you know yourself. If you tend to overheat during blizzards, maybe you can pack less layers. If you're like that couple I met in an elevator in San Diego, wearing matching quilted polar fleece jackets with price tags still on them, plan on bundling up. They said they live in Florida, and were freezing, although I found the 87-degree day delightful.

Worried about seasickness? I've been on many cruises, and yes, the Gulf of Alaska does have more waves than some milder places. Cruises in the Caribbean barely have a ripple, much less a wave. In fact, when we took a trans-Atlantic cruise on a ship repositioning from a season in the mild Caribbean, over two hundred *crew members and officers* lined up that first evening for a shot of something to quell seasickness. I didn't think the ship was rolling much, but after feeling no waves at all for four months, it hit them hard. We passengers could have been more sympathetic, I suppose.

In Alaska, storms and waves are common, more so in the Gulf of Alaska, less in the Inside Passage. If you're prone to sea sickness, wearing a sea band or a patch is a good idea. See *Tips From The Cruise Addict's Wife* for a lengthy list of tips and remedies that can head off seasickness. Did you know it's hereditary?

Even if you're not the kind to get seasick, do be aware of your surroundings any time the ship is moving, especially in the bathroom. It's not easy, Husband says, shaving a face that sways in the mirror, and I can attest to the ineffectiveness of holding onto a shower handrail with a soapy hand during a storm. Be aware that outer decks may be closed for safety if winds grow too stiff. Besides sandblasting your face, it can be dangerous.

In rough seas, children often manage better than grown-ups. We traveled to Alaska with our one-year-old granddaughter, and she did better than anyone else onboard. When the waves in the Gulf of Alaska rocked the boat, adults couldn't walk a straight line. I chuckled, coming out of the theatre one evening, watching the crowd sway a couple of steps to the left, then to the right, as if choreographed. Our granddaughter was the only one walking normally, a factor of her very low center of gravity. Plus, she hadn't been walking very long, and was used to compensating for feeling unsteady on her feet.

Don't let weather deter you, however. One of my favorite memories is of my whole family together in the pool in 80-knot winds while glaciers slid past the ship. It was a full-on wave pool!

What to buy in Alaska?

For many tourists, a souvenir is a good way to bring home a memory of their travels. In just about every cruise port around the western hemisphere, you will find the same stores: the one with the stuff that changes colors in the sunshine, Caribbean jewelry stores offering the same gemstones, etc. Alaska has those, too, many owned by the cruise lines themselves. I suggest you walk on by and seek authentic local shops that offer some fine items including local art, native crafts, unique foods, and things you just don't see everywhere else.

Summer is cruise season in Alaska, and the port towns rely heavily on the income tourists bring on cruises, both from shopping, tours, and the steep port fees passed on to passengers. Most towns cannot supply enough sales clerks to man the stores when the flood of passenrs surge down the cruise ships' gangways. They hire clerks, mostly college students, from the lower forty-eight to man the shops through the cruise season. Fall college semesters begin around the same time cruise ships head for warmer climes, making a win-win for the townspeople, who return to their quieter lives once the flurry passes, and the students, who leave with full pockets.

If you're interested in cheesy trinkets like mugs, shot glasses, magnets, and cutesy kissing Eskimo salt and pepper shakers, they're everywhere, along with Alaska-themed toys, tee shirts, sweatshirts, and caps. Nothing wrong with a moose hand puppet or a stuffed sled dog, after all. You might like a little totem pole or Alaka-themed ornament for your Christmas tree to remember your cruise.

Most likely, you'll want an ulu on your first trip to Alaska. So many people buy ulu; they're a best-seller. An ulu is a very sharp kitchen knife with a curved blade and a handle on top, designed to be used in a rocking motion. Some are sold with shallow bamboo bowls, although bamboo isn't native to Alaska. In the hand of someone who knows what they're doing, ulu can be almost as fast as a food processor! Inexpensive wood-handled ulu cost under $5, while carved bone-handled models run closer to $80.

Ulu are sharp, and cruise lines consider them weapons. On most lines, the knives will be confiscated as you reboard the ship and returned to you the last night of your cruise...functionally arming the whole ship for a few hours. Don't think about it. Remember to pack them in your checked luggage, rather than your carry-on, for the flight home, because airlines have no sense of humor about blades on planes. Pack the local honey, jams, and syrups in your checked baggage, too, or the TSA guys will make you throw it away at the airport.

I'm still sore about TSA confiscating my hastily-packed maple syrup I bought right at the maple processing place in Halifax, NB. Yes, I should have watched Husband to be sure he packed it anywhere but my carry on, after The Incident, but I still suspect the agents' taking my syrup had less to do with National Security and more to do with his breakfast the following morning. It was the good stuff, I tell you.

Oh, The Incident? If you're looking for a life lesson, let it be to keep an eye on your traveling companion. In this case, it was the Cruise Addict, alias Husband. We were in an airport security line on our way to...I forget where. We travel rather a lot. He reached into his pocket to remove his keys, coins, phone, and stuff that could set off the metal detector yet again. He has a pattern of being pulled aside for extra screening, which is both time consuming and annoying. This time, he felt his pocket knife in the depths of his khakis! Absentmindedly, he'd slipped it in his pocket, and you know the security folks would raise a fuss.

Well, an hour later, on the plane, I reached into my very own personal carry on, and pulled out his knife! I turned on him, furious; had there been An Issue, it would have been ME they came after! His defense? "You didn't know you had it in your bag, so your face looked innocent." I spent the flight alternately fuming at him for setting me up to get in trouble, and wondering how many other people on the plane had a weapon at hand.

Along with locally made jams and syrups, what else should you look for in Alaska? I believe in Being Where You Are, so no mass-produced, made-in-China stuff for me. I seek authentic Made In Alaska items. They're easy to spot; they have a label right on them.

You might like to bring home a bit of Alaskan culture. Native Alaska cultural items can be pricey, including button blankets, native artwork and masks, ulu, and anything made of musk ox wool, but most items have a decent price range.

Ceremonial masks and totem poles are native to coastal Alaska, where cruise ships pull into dock. Small scale totem poles in varying sizes and materials, from hand-carved wood to polymer resin models are available in every port, with prices ranging from $2 to about $40 for a larger one. Two-story hand-carved wooden totems are significantly higher, and delivery can be a hassle. Anything that big won't fit in your suitcase.

Masks may be made of wood, whalebone, or caribou skin, often hand-painted. Authentic spirit wheels and dream catchers bring together the physical and spiritual worlds, and are a great conversation piece at home. You can find locally-made baskets, antler carvings, and drums at many tourist shops, while better quality ones can be found in galleries sprinkled through the ports.

Paintings depicting wildlife or scenes of traditional Alaskan life are often stunningly detailed. Those long Alaskan winters leave time to develop a talent. It's worth your time to visit a gallery, even if your home décor doesn't lend itself to this style. Truly talented artists live in the Great Land, and you should at least admire their work.

If you collect dolls, the Made-in-Alaska figures in native dress will steal your heart. Dressed in intricate furs and tanned hides, they're art on a small scale. Prices start at about $150. If you're looking for a toy a child can play with, the mass-produced dolls are closer to $35, and easily found in many stores. Unfortunately, they tend to have white skin — not exactly an authentic look. I'm still puzzled over seeing so many blonde baby dolls in Mexico, too!

Anything made of musk ox wool (knit or crocheted) is going to be expensive: think $200 for a pair of handmade gloves. Musk ox are wild, not the kind of animal you can walk up and sheer like a calm, domestic sheep, and finding their fluffy wool isn't easy! In the springtime, musk ox shed their thick winter coats, snagging tufts of the soft stuff on tundra and branches as they pass by. Dedicated wool-gatherers (not the day-dreaming kind) trek miles, stuffing clumps of shed fuzz into bags. Their payoff? They get to see the bouncy baby musk oxen cavorting on the tundra.

A shopping tip: if you happen to book a cruise late in the season, watch for great sale prices in most shops in every port. Store owners would rather sell items, even at a loss, than store them until the next summer. Markdowns of up to 90% are not uncommon. Pay attention to what you buy, even at that price. Sure, you look fine onboard in your new grizzly-bear-themed fleece jacket, but will you really wear it to the office once you're back home?

Embarkation Ports:

While some longer cruises begin in California, the majority of Alaskan cruises begin in Seattle or Vancouver, British Columbia, making a round trip loop. A second option is a one-way cruise from Vancouver to Anchorage, or the opposite route. Obviously, those go further north than ones that stay in Southeast Alaska. With one-way cruises, travelers can opt to book a cruise-tour into the heart of Alaska and Denali National Park. You could even tack another full Alaska cruise back-to-back on the end of your cruise if you choose. Each itinerary includes stops at small towns along the way, and at least one tidewater glacier. Let's look at advantages and downfalls of each option. I like choices, don't you?

Cruises that say they begin or end on Anchorage are...misrepresenting. Only a handful of cruises venture up the Cook Inlet into Anchorage. It adds at least another day or more onto any itinerary, so most opt to begin or end in of two towns near Anchorage: Whittier or Seward. Both are connected to Anchorage by road and rail, and the scenery is lovely. I saw my first beluga whales there, rolling like white-playdough-colored beach balls in the sound. They looked rather unfinished to me.

Whittier is about 60 miles southeast of Anchorage, a drive of roughly an hour and a half. Seward is about a three-hour drive southeast of Anchorage, on the Kenai Peninsula. Many cruise lines include transportation from these ports to Anchorage as part of their cruise fare, or you can book a shore excursion that'll take you from the ship to the city, with a few interesting stops along the way.

The round-trip cruises leave from Seattle or Vancouver. Both have major airports and Amtrak links them both, but there are some differences.

Seattle: More than half of Alaska's cruises start in the Emerald City, so named because of the very green scenery, dominated by towering cedars and other evergreens. I find it funny when newcomers comment on how beautiful Seattle is, how lush, how green! They often visit during the summer, when the weather can be temperate (unless summer is canceled, and I swear it feels like that some years!). They have no concept of what it takes to sustain that much green scenery...it rains All. The. Time.

Seattle gets less rain than, say, Houston, but in Texas, it knows how to properly rain. Rain hard, then stop. In Seattle, we get many dark, grey, gloomy days of rain, and we certainly complain about it. Actually, *many* places log more rain that we get here. It's not really even raindrops; more of a thick mist-drizzle, a mizzle, where you don't need to turn the windshield wipers on and you can't see where you're going if they're off. However, during the short summers, Seattle is lovely, and there's much to do and see.

A couple of tips: everybody wants to see the iconic Space Needle. The rule is, if you can see the top of it clearly, go ahead. On a cloudy or overcast day, you're wasting your money. Speaking of money, nearby Columbia Center's elevator whisks people 73 stories up for a few dollars less than the Space Needle, and is usually not as crowded. The Space Needle will undergo a major renovation starting in 2018, adding more glass, more elevators, more views, more seating, and ...well, just *more*.

Seattle is one of the busiest seaports on the west coast, with massive container ships coming from Asia and South America in a never-ending stream. The harbor itself is pretty. If you are there long enough, you might consider taking a harbor cruise, just for the scenery.

Two piers are designated for cruise ships. Bell Street Terminal at Pier 66 is close to downtown, an easy walk from Seattle Aquarium and Pike Place Market, unless you're lugging suitcases. Carnival, Celebrity, and Norwegian cruise lines use Pier 66, along with Ocean Cruises. The ships draw envious glances, glistening in Elliott Bay.

Parking in Seattle is pricey no matter where you go, but the across-the-street facility by Pier 66 caters to cruise passengers, even picking up luggage near your car and transporting it to the ship for you. It also offers luggage holds, which can be handy after the cruise if you're hankering to explore the city before your flight home, unencumbered by baggage.

Smith Cove Terminal, at Pier 91 north of Seattle, is home to Holland America Line, Princess Cruises, and Royal Caribbean Cruise Line. There isn't much within walking distance of Pier 91, but the main part of the city is just a short cab ride away. The terminus is handicap accessible, and has fairly smooth traffic flow for both vehicles and pedestrians, so long as you keep an eye on the signs.

If you're driving in, double check your GSP navigator system. Mine led me on a wild goose chase through narrow, winding residential areas on Queen Anne Hill, then stopped at a cliff and smugly announced, "You have arrived at your destination." Far down below, I saw the ship, and from that distance, it looked about five inches end to end. My destination? I don't think so.

Seatac is Seattle's international airport, located 30 and 45 minutes by cab from the cruise piers, respectively. If you can fly in a day or more early, you'll find Seattle a tourist-friendly city. You won't run out of things to do. Take in a ballgame or concert, visit the Chihuly Glass Museum, ride a ferry, enjoy the Science Center or the Boeing Museum of Flight near Seatac Airport. If you come in a few days early, consider renting a car and driving north or east. The Cascade Loop is a beautiful two-day drive, through high desert, the Cascade Mountains, Washington's orchards and vineyards, even a Bavarian-style village. I like stopping at the Apple Visitors Center for a sample of apple varietals that aren't even on the market yet. Washington is known for apples, you know.

Seattle cruise itineraries almost always skirt Vancouver Island, heading into the open sea as soon as they pass the Straits of Juan de Fuca, on up into the Gulf of Alaska. They may stop at Victoria on the way. Because ships leaving Seattle don't enter the Inside Passage until north of Vancouver Island, you'll have a day or two of lazy at-sea sailing. Some people relish that down time, making the most of shipboard activities and resting after their trip from home. It's a time to explore the ship and get your bearings. Scenery is still visible on the east side of the ship, fjorns, peaks, and all. Watch for improbably small crab and fishing boats tossed on the wide open sea.

Vancouver, British Columbia, located about three hours north of Seattle by car, is the second busiest jump-off point for cruises to Alaska, both round-trip and one-way. Canada Place is the pier for Carnival, Royal Caribbean, Princess Cruises, Holland America Cruise Lines, plus the more upscale Regent Seven Seas, Oceana, SilverSea, and Seabourne cruise lines.

Canada Place is on the edge of downtown. Since all the cruise lines go to the one pier, back-to-back cruising is really easy. Several times, I've disembarked one ship, walked across the pier and boarded another ship. So long as it's on a different cruise line to get past that old archaic law, go for it.

However, Canada Place is known for its slow boarding process, and can become overwhelmed when too many ships are in port all at once. Long lines can rival the back-and-forth ones at Disneyland. Our record wait was five hours twenty minutes to get through Customs. The ship left hours late, and with every announcement onboard, I could hear the captain's irritation increasing. Behind the scenes, I'm pretty sure heads were rolling. If your cruise is one of several in port on the same day, I recommend packing a snack. And some patience!

On especially hectic days, a cruise ship or two can be docked at the commercial shipping port a couple of miles away. That rarely happens, and it's a good thing, because it's not designed for passengers. The few times I've ended up there, security was so tight that departing passengers were walked down the gangway and directly onto a bus, ten feet from the ramp, and transported to the Convention Center a few blocks from Canada Place. They call it Convention *Centre,* but you know what I mean.

Again, if you can swing it, go to Vancouver a day or more before your cruise. Not only will you skip the frantic anxiety of worrying about a flight delay making you miss sailaway, you'll have a chance to enjoy this beautiful city. Vancouver is one of my favorite places...so long as I'm not driving my car. The road rules are, shall we say, random. The roads' lanes change from roadway to parking slots depending on the time of day, the day of the week, and some higher-up's whims, as far as I can tell. Canadians are known for being a calm, mellow people, but even Canadians avoid driving in Vancouver if they can help it. Legendary, and not in a good way.

Vancouver-ites had the foresight to build a convenient transit system of buses and a monorail called the Skytrain. It opened in 1986, on time and under budget; no easy task. Skytrain is easy to use, fun to ride, and goes to the major city areas for a reasonable price. Purchase tickets at the kiosks located at each stop. Yes, you do have to buy them, even though it looks as though no one will ever know if you just step on the Skytrain. When they do random checks, you need to show a ticket. Trust me: you can't afford the fine, which is much higher than your standard overdue library book fee. Read the route map carefully; the zone you purchase may include the water taxi or buses as well.

I think it's pretty safe; I took 26 Brownies on a four-day trip to Vancouver a while ago and we rode the Skytrain all over the place. I didn't even lose any of the little girls, a feat I'm pretty proud of. Children can be pretty squirrely at that age.

Vancouver International Airport is about 35 minutes from the heart of downtown, where the port at Canada Place is located. If you're flying from an American city, you might want to compare prices. Often, flying to Seattle then taking Amtrak to Vancouver will save a significant amount, plus you'll get to enjoy the leisurely train ride north. Be sure to request a "water side" seat; the scenery is much better. Amtrak ends at Union Station, within eyesight of a Skytrain stop, and Skytrain takes people to within a block of Canada Place. If you have a lot of luggage to wrangle, you may find it easier to just grab a cab at the station.

Unlike the cruise route from Seattle, ships sailing from Canada Place stay behind Vancouver Island, along the coastline. There's more opportunities for wildlife-spotting early on, but less chance of seeing whales at first. If you worry about getting seasick, you might be happier leaving from Vancouver, where the waters tend to be very calm. There are two spots— one at the northern rim of Vancouver Island

and the other at the tip of the Queen Charlotte Islands—where you can have some rough water, but it's no more than a few hours in each case.

If your cruise sails from Vancouver, you'll be in the Inside Passage pretty much the whole route. Scenery is lovely, with land visible on both sides of the ship for at least a few days, so close you could hit it with a baseball, and not even a Major League pitch.

If your cruise ends in Vancouver and you have time on your hands, your first stop should be the Vancouver Tourism Centre, right across the street from the terminal. They'll offer advice on what to see, and give you a nice walking map. If the weather's fine, you'd enjoy a lazy walk along the seawall, or out to Stanley Park...although, I warn you, it's farther than it looks! The seawall is thirteen miles long; you don't have to cover all of it. Vancouver has markets and interesting stores as well as a vibrant arts scene that comes alive during summer months.

Vancouver is known as "Hollywood North" due to many movies and television shows that are filmed on location there. Several times, I've stopped to watch filming: so long as you're silent and stay out of the way, no one minds. I found the process fascinating, especially the use of extras. A man in a baseball cap walked into the "San Francisco Courthouse" behind the main character. He looped through another door, out of the camera's view, took off the cap, picked up a briefcase and a coffee cup, then walked across the set, intent on his cell phone. Passing behind the camera, he donned a trench coat and took the hand of a young actor carrying a shopping bag, walking past the main character who was still in conversation. The man morphed into four different characters in under two minutes. Not something I see every day!

Anchorage

If your cruise says it starts or ends in Anchorage, look closer. Cruises ships don't like to waste time and fuel going around the Kenai Peninsula, so you'll most likely go to either Seward or Whittier, then transport to Anchorage. Most cruise lines include this transfer in the cruise fare, since it's not smart to leave 2000+ passengers stranded in these tiny towns on a weekly basis. If you disdain the cruise line's motor coach, you can easily book an Alaskan Railway trip on your own, or add in a private tour of Portage Glacier on your way.

If you can afford an extra few days either before or after your cruise, Anchorage is a prime place to spend them! Besides being the city where most inland land tours begin, there's plenty to do right there in town.

First, stop and breathe. Anchorage is a major city, but it has a feeling all its own, not conducive to just rushing through without paying attention. About 300,000 people have Anchorage addresses, but they're so spread out, you may not notice. Anchorage is Alaska's largest city, both in population and size on a map. Yet, it lacks the hustle-and-bustle frenzy of other big cities. I stood in the middle of the busiest intersection in downtown Anchorage at 11 am on an ordinary August Monday morning, and counted a total of eight cars in a ten minute period. Rush hour? Traffic jam? What's that?

What they lack in cars, they make up in small planes. Anchorage is the world's busiest seaplane port. Victoria, BC comes in second; your cruise might stop there, too. Anchorage is a perfect combination of a commercial center and natural beauty. Yes, you'll find a few tall buildings, but during the winter, it's not uncommon for a hungry moose to meander right through downtown, looking for a snack. They've been known to munch Christmas decorations right off houses' front doors, if they have those tasty red berries on them!

Don't miss the Alaska Native Heritage Center in Anchorage for a fine overview of the local culture, which isn't anything like the rest of the United States at all. The Anchorage Museum is a must-see, a comprehensive collection of Alaska artifacts on permanent loan from the Smithsonian Institution. A photo op with the life-sized bronze moose downtown is nearly required. It's like posing as if you're pushing up the Leaning Tower of Pisa. You, and 7000 other people, have the same photo. There's room for you, too.

Take a cab to the Alaska Aviation Museum, about eight miles out of town on the south shore of Lake Hood. Loaded with interactive displays, memorabilia, photographs and artifacts from the personal collections of Alaska's pioneer aviators... And pioneers they were! Did you know Alaska has its own version of the Bermuda Triangle? Every year, several small planes vanish. The mountains give up some of them, often years later, but many are never found. Don't gloss over the courage of the bush pilots, both in history and today.

If you're still craving wildlife, plan a visit to the Alaska Zoo, the Alaska Wildlife Conservation Center, or book a tour to Redoubt Bay, where bears hang out during summer months.

Cruise Ports And What To Do There

Alaskan ports aren't the only ones you'll visit. More than likely, your cruise will stop at one or more Canadian cities. Victoria or Vancouver are common ports, but your itinerary may include Prince Rupert, Nanaimo, or another small city as well. Wherever it is, take time to soak up the local flavor.

Victoria is the capital of British Columbia, with a distinctly British feel. Cruise ships dock a couple of miles from downtown. Cruise lines offer shuttles, or you can catch a cab, limo or hackney rickshaw right there at the pier. On a nice day, you might choose to walk, at least half way. The path is well-marked, not too hilly, and quite pleasant. When you reach Fisherman's Wharf, you can walk on around the bend to downtown, but I suggest taking a water taxi. They're little enclosed boats, capacity under ten, that whisk passengers across the harbor to the cayside. It's lovely, inexpensive, and gives a nice perspective on the city.

Burdened with history, Victoria also has a lively nightlife, a brisk public market, and many street performers on sunny afternoons. They're called "buskers," a British term I bet you don't use every day.

The Royal BC Museum is one of the finest I've seen (and I know my museums!). Located across the street from the lofty Empress Hotel and the Parliament Building, it's easy to locate and well worth your time. The Parliament Building is open during business hours for both guided tours as well as self-guided wandering, and at dusk, it's outlined with over 3300 lights. You might enjoy the wax museum, Miniature World, or exploring the elegant Empress Hotel.

Prince Rupert, British Columbia is mighty proud of its moniker, the "Halibut Capital Of The World." Located on the deepest harbor in North America, it's reputed to be one of the oldest continuously occupied regions in the world, although it never really took off, size-wise. Small, interesting museums and artist studios can be found, but the main two things to do in Prince Rupert are to go fishing or eat fish and chips. Try the halibut; it's delicious!

Chances are, your cruise will only be in the town a short time. I enjoy simply walking through the quiet streets. It's on the edge of a rain forest, and I was drenched one day when I left my poncho on the cruise ship. I shower daily, but I don't get any wetter than I did that day. Seeking refuge in a nice dry firehouse, I struck up a conversation with a couple of the friendliest people I've met anywhere. Don't hesitate to speak to locals.

Nanaimo is another port many cruise ships visit. Its claim to fame is the Nanaimo Bar, a decadent, gooey sweet that's half cookie, half candy, and entirely yummy. Available at over 35 venues in town, they're easy to find and hard to resist. Sample at least one Nanaimo Bar, then walk off those calories along the seaside. Looking out over the panoramic mountain views and busy harbor, you'll forget all those silly things like your day planner, schedule, deadlines, and other stressors waiting for you at home.

Nanaimo is Vancouver Island's second-largest city, but maintains a small-town feel. Stop by the Tourism Nanaimo desk in the terminal building for advice on a walking tour and other things to do. At the least, check out the Bastion. You'll hear cannon fire and bagpipes at noon, overlooking the bustling market. Local snacks and handmade wares abound, offered by friendly vendors.

Interested in a more sedate shopping experience? Nanaimo features three distinct shopping districts: The Old City Quarter up the hill, the Arts District downtown, and the Waterfront District, along the Harborfront Walkway. Often, the mayor of the town will be on hand to greet every cruise ship, with Mounties available for photos. Did you know Mounties wear scarlet skivvies as a part of their uniform?

Alaska Ports

For many people, the best part of Alaskan cruises is the cruising itself, with every-changing scenery and the chance to spot wildlife right over the rail. Nevertheless, ports along your cruise route each have their own character, and each is well worth exploring. Step into visitor's centers, small museums, and take advantage of the parks' offerings. Sample local foods while you're there- you're making memories!

Some of the ports on an Alaskan cruise itinerary are quite small, and easily overwhelmed by multiple cruise ships disgorging a few thousand eager passengers, each. To avoid crowds of tourists in any port, simply walk inland a few blocks. Eighty percent of tourists stay in ten percent of any port's area. I don't know why; but it's true worldwide. Once you move slightly away from the port, you'll get a real feel for the town and its residents.

Take time to explore off-the-beaten-path shops, small restaurants, old cemeteries (the Russian one in Sitka is lovely), even stop in the local library. Libraries in Alaska are surprisingly well-used, and offer free wi-fi as well as a place to rest while perusing local newspapers. Plus, the librarians tend to be good at pointing people to historical places they'd otherwise overlook.

Take time to chat with local residents: shop owners, waiters, cabbies, all of them. Many of them have fascinating stories to tell, like the man in Ketchikan who commissioned an artist in nearby Hydatown to make his wife a full-sized totem pole for her birthday, and planted it in their front yard. You're not in Kansas anymore.

It's a sad world-view to think that the only interesting things and people are in your home town. Expand your horizons on your cruise, and take in some local color wherever you can. You may have Native American culture at home, but not like Alaska has.

Clans define a person; it's common for an introduction to include a person's name and clan. There are lines one simply does not cross, especially with regards to marriage. As a tourist, you're not likely to run into any taboo, but be aware that local culture is very big in Alaska.

There are a couple dozen major native cultures in Alaska, divided and defined by language. The three main ones in Southeast

Alaska, where cruise ships ply the waters, are Tlingit, Haida, and Tsimshian. Losing their "old ways" culture is a battle many fight as new influences swamp communities, and these tribes are no different. Recently, the last couple of decades, an emphasis on preserving culture and language has been a priority.

Recently realizing that only a handful (10-35!) living people spoke the old languages fluently, now it's taught in local schools, along with dance, carving, and subsistence skills such as fishing and drying salmon. In some ports, including Ketchikan and Sitka, local dancers perform for tourists, hoping to keep the dances alive, while providing an opportunity for the younger generation to learn the old ways. I was saddened to overhear some cruise passengers comment derisively, "I didn't come all this way to watch somebody's kid dress up in feathers and dance!" They completely missed witnessing the magic of the art passing down through generations.

Ketchikan is located on the edge of the Tongass National Forest, the nation's largest. The prideful little town bills itself as Alaska's First City (because it's often the first Alaskan port, coming from the south) and The Salmon Capital of the World. A small fishing town, Ketchikan clings to its lively past like cockleburs on new wool socks. Take time to absorb it! It's one of my favorite places on earth.

Pick up a walking tour map at the visitor's center, or download a pdf before you leave home. Creek Street is a nod to its not-very-distant past as a legal Red Light district. The bars and bordellos were built on stilts over the creek, and each had a trap door to hide illicit liquor stores in case of a raid during Prohibition. They're converted to colorful little shops these days. Take time or read the historic markers on your quest for souvenirs along the wooden walkway over the creek. And don't forget to look in the water! When salmon are running in late summertime, the water is black with salmon, all bumping and crushing on their way to the fish ladder. Can't say the smell is wonderful, but it's amazing to see.

Ketchikan is in a rain forest, with only about a hundred days a year having no measurable rain. The 7,000 or so year-round residents of Ketchikan measure rainfall in feet - over *fifteen* feet - rather than inches, giving Ketchikan the reputation of the rainiest place in Alaska. Yes, I still complain about Seattle's rain. Dress in layers: I've been there on 85-degree days, as well as during a monsoon, otherwise known as Tuesday. Don't let a little sky water deter you; you're going to love Ketchikan!

Southeast Alaska Discovery Center is one of the best-presented centers I've seen - and I seek out these places when I travel. You'll find yourself immersed in local culture, fishing and gold-seeking history, in a non-lecture-y way. The cultural videos offered are worth well the few extra minutes. It's within easy walking distance of the port.

Ever ridden a funicular? It's a car that clings to the steep hillside above Ketchikan. It costs about $3 to go up (free to locals) and it's free to ride back down, if you choose. It's worth it for the view alone. The Cape Fox Inn at the top has a nice display of local artifacts on the mezzanine level. Head out back to see the circle of totem poles. Ketchikan has the most concentrated collection of totem poles in the Northwest; if you're interested in totems, now's your chance! A few times, I've seen bear warnings posted on the door there, but don't let that stop you. They're just looking for food, and people don't taste that great, so I've heard.

Around to the left of the building, a sidewalk hugging the hotel leads to a wooden walkway, the famed Married Man's trail, used in early days when bars on Creek Street were raided, sending men who feared being caught lingering in brothels scattering. The walk is fairly easy, with a couple of flights of stairs and a few steep parts, but it's wide and has good handrails. And scenic, a really pretty walk, and besides, you have to go back down the hill one way or another.

You'll pass by the rapids of the creek, where the salmon jump up the waterfalls trying to reach their spawning grounds. Those fish are tough, leaping up rushing water many time their height in an effort to reach their home turf, miles upstream.

You'll reach a fork partway down, where you can either continue down to Creek Street, or follow the trail to the right. Signs point to the Deer Mountain Salmon Hatchery and Totem Heritage Cultural Center. The Center is interesting! Many totem poles from all around Alaska are housed there, but don't expect to see the flashy, painted ones found elsewhere; this is preserved history.

 The first time we visited the Center, a carver invited me to a potlatch the following weekend. I'm still disappointed: that was perhaps the only time I've considered deliberately missing a ship at sailaway. Oh, and again in Greece, but that was for a different reason. Greece has no totem poles, but I was invited to an olive oil pressing on a family farm, and that's not an invitation I'll ever see again. I digress.

The Great Alaskan Lumberjack show is great fun, as well as offering an insight into the skills a lumberjack used in time past. The competitive show will have you laughing, clapping, and cheering on your team. They really are amazing; I watched a logger carve a child's chair using a chainsaw in under a minute flat! And I gained a new respect for Husband. He was invited to participate in an ax-throwing contest. Who knew the Cruise Addict could hit a bull's eye at fifty paces with an ax? Walking around Ketchikan, you can often hear the cheers from the show. It's a nice break from the rain, if any happens to be falling. The outdoor seats are under cover, with heaters.

Venturing further afield, consider Saxman Village or Totem Bight Park. Saxman is located seven miles out of town. The full show is only available to cruise ship shore excursion groups, one of the very few times I recommend buying a tour through the cruise line. Part of the rather steep fee goes to maintain the village itself, as well as to promote the native culture and languages of nearby tribes. Some people say they disdained native dances performed by school children, but how will traditions be preserved if they are not passed along to the next generation?

Low-key Totem Bight park can be reached by local bus in about an hour, faster by taxi. Download a walking tour guide before you go so you'll know what the totem poles represent. It's no fun looking at something, puzzling what on earth the artist intended to depict.

Haines is a recent addition to some Alaskan itineraries. With a population of under two thousand on a good day, Haines confidently bills itself as the Adventure Capital of the World. One of our cruises was unable to make the port in Skagway due to 80-knot winds rushing through the narrow fork. That'd be a hurricane anywhere else, but Alaskans took it in stride. Our captain announced we'd make an unscheduled stop in Haines instead.

Ignoring the grumbles about missing shore excursions, we set out to enjoy Haines...and we had a great afternoon! A horse-drawn wagon ride gave us an overview of the town, narrated by a resident who pointed out eagle aeries, overnight bear damage, and boasted about Alaska's heli-ski rescue center, located in Haines. We explored the thriving artist community, then attended a storyteller's presentation. I thoroughly enjoyed hearing local legends told by a skilled tale-weaver.

Because the ship was in port just a couple of hours, we missed the Hammer Museum, the only such place in the world dedicated to the oldest tool used by humans. The Alaska-Chilkat Bald Eagle Preserve is located near the town as well. I'm not sure I'd make a special trip to see Haines, but if you're heartset, take the high-speed ferry from Skagway.

Skagway

Skagway manages to preserve a good bit of its gold rush flavor, and it's a fine jump-off point into the Yukon. Speaking of flavor, Skagway is known for having the most varieties of colored popcorn in North America. Odd claim to fame, but there you are.

Skagway is one of my favorite ports, worldwide. The spirit of the gold seeker, the hardy (some say "fool hardy") souls who braved the harsh winters feeding their gold fever, and the, shall we say, *entrepreneurs,* whose goals were to mine the miners for their gold, burned their hopeful courage into the town's very earth. Early history is all around, in the very air.

As you walk the boardwalk on your way to the next souvenir shop, notice the storefronts. Most of them are original, from soon after Skagway was settled. The Chilkoot Pass towers over town, a stark reminder of the fearless gold-seekers who left all they had to stake their claim. Right on the Pack Train Building, a stern reminder lingers: **U-AU-To-No-The-Trail** in wooden letters.

One of the best souvenir shops is located in Skagway, if you're interested in that sort of thing. Head down the boardwalk. The last store on the right at the end of the boardwalk offers the lowest prices I've seen in Alaska for pretty much the same stuff sold in each port. And it's right across the street from a mighty fine fudge shop.

The Arctic Brotherhood Hall is reputed to be the most photographed building in Alaska, although I have no idea who tracks such data. In times past, it was a fraternal hall; the local chapter of the

Brotherhood first met here in August 1899. Step across the street, and you'll notice the letters "A.B." and the "1899" above the door, and "Camp Skagway No. 1" on the overhang. The organization's symbol, a gold pan and nuggets, is up near the roof line.

The facade, which dates from 1900, has been called "a prime example of Victorian Rustic Architecture." You may find it just plain whimsical. Charley Walker and his fellow lodge members collected 8,883 driftwood sticks on the shores of Skagway Bay and... nailed them to the front wall. No one knows why; Alaska affects people in different ways. The building is currently the home of the tiny Visitor Information Center.

Remember *The Legend of Sam McGee?* It's a rollicking poem/ballad, worth looking up when you get a chance. It was based on a long Skagway winter. You've heard of Soapy Smith, the Bad Guys' Bad Guy, haven't you? One of the most notorious (and creative) scoundrels, old Soapy took over Skagway during the winter of 1897-98. Through a combination of charm, skill, and guile, he soon controlled an underworld of more than two hundred gamblers, swindlers, and thugs.

The "Days of '98" show, a melodrama in downtown Skagway, is a delightful way to spend an hour. You'll laugh, sing along, and pick up some history while you're there. The actors are available for photo ops after the show. I found myself in an eye-opening conversation with Old Soapy himself, played by a high school teacher. You never know what tidbits you might learn, just by speaking to someone!

One caution: before the show, one of the "fancy ladies" will ask for a volunteer from the audience. Don't let that be you. Not only does the victim miss a good part of the melodrama, the resulting phots by friends and family are prime blackmail material!

I highly recommend stopping at the Klondike Gold Rush National Historic Park Service building in Skagway, and joining one of the walking tours offered. They're free, last under an hour, and offer a wonderful glimpse into history. One of the rangers we met was a skilled weaver of tales, so much so that I quoted her in my Alaskan cruise novel, **Murder On Deck**. In this excerpt, the characters are participating in a walking tour offered by the Parks Service:

The small group stopped in front of a small wooden building. "This was the slick, fast-talking, low-life flimflammer's office, where much of his nefarious dealings went on. His main occupation was mining the gold miners, making money off them any way he could devise, and he was a sly one."

"One thing the homesick prospectors were desperate for was communication with the folks at home. That scoundrel set up a telegraph system, charging exorbitant fees for messages sent, paid in gold up front. Of course, the telegraph operator was one of his men, and he wrote down and dutifully keyed in the precious messages. If the miners told their kinfolk they were bust, they sent them on their way. But if a miner sent word home that he'd found gold, Soapy's men would follow the prospector to his claim, and I don't mean for afternoon tea."

"Either way, the cost of sending a message home was outrageous." She pointed to an exposed wire protruding from the roofline. "And as you can see, it was no system at all, just another of Soapy's scams. The messages didn't reach back east; they barely cleared the roof."

"Poor people, to be that desperate, and with little recourse!" a woman choked out.

The ranger agreed. "Skagway and Dyea were a long way from the delicate city life most prospectors left to seek the gleam of gold, and bad actors were abundant. Soapy Smith's power seemed almost limitless until July 8, 1898, when the townspeople finally had enough. Surveyor Frank Reid lured the old charlatan into a trap, and they ended up shooting it out on one of the town's docks.

Skagway only has a handful of cars for rent, but if you can reserve one way in advance, driving up into the Yukon will change your life. Save that for a subsequent cruise; Skagway has plenty to offer on its own for a first-timer.

Sitka

Ketchikan *calls* itself the first city, but Sitka actually *is*. The signing of the Alaskan purchase (aka Seward's Folly) took place on Castle Hill in Sitka. The strong Russian influence lingers, in architecture, wares, language, and the cemetery.

The former Russian capital of North America, Sitka is the only city in Southeast Alaska to touch the Pacific Ocean; the others are on the Gulf of Alaska. Seward's Folly is also known as "Seward's Icebox" was the derisive nickname given to the Purchase of Alaska in 1867. Purchasing the tract from Russia cost the

US government a resounding four cents an acre. Obviously, somebody failed to note the wealth of natural resources.

Sitka is rich in history and natural beauty. It served as the state capital of Alaska until 1906, when the economy of the city faltered and seat of government was transferred to Juneau.

The gold rush of 1849 actually began months earlier in Sitka; it took a while for word to reach civilization. Silver Bay marks the spot where a rich gold vein was discovered, simply by somebody turning over a rock. There's plenty of gold still in Alaska; it's just not very cost-effective to mine it on a large-scale basis right now. A few large mines do remain; a family member works in the largest.

 If you take a few minutes to pan any stream in Alaska, you're likely to find at least a few flecks of the gleaming metal. Want a tip? Gold is heavy, and swirling water currents push it into eddies and crevices, as well as behind rocks. In just a few minutes in almost any stream, you can find a few flakes. That, and $5, will buy a burger in town.

You'll find the hop-on-hop-off bus (a van) near the cruise terminal. For $10, you can ride all day and see the main highlights of the town, getting on and off as you wish. The HOHO runs only when 10,000 or more people are in town. That may sound like a lot, but that's the population of only two or three cruise ships. I saw a cruise ship calendar that showed at least one cruise ship-and up to six!- scheduled to stop in Sitka every single day from May through September.

The New Archangel Dancers are unique to Sitka, and well worth seeing. The talent is excellent, as are the authentic cultural dances performed, but don't gloss over their back story. In 1970, a group of women wanted to start a dance group to preserve the Russian folk dances and culture. The men in town scoffed and mocked, refusing to join in. So, the women danced both male and female parts. Several years later, when the men saw how successful the venture was, they begged to participate. The women firmly told them, "You had your chance." The New Archangel Dancers is an all-female troupe to this day. The performances are held whenever cruise ships are in town, and randomly during summer months.

Sitka is a world-class fishing destination. It boasts the shortest rod-hour-to-catch ratio for King salmon in the entire state of Alaska. That means, unless you forget to bait your hook, you'll catch a fish. If you dream of landing an Alaska salmon, this is a great place. Tour operators will process, freeze, and ship the fish back home for you. Sitka sits directly on the open ocean, so you can go after all five species of Pacific salmon in an easy outing from Sitka.

A few miles from Sitka, on Admiralty Island, is the location of the Fortress of the Bears. A reserve for endangered Alaskan bears, it's an opportunity to see the giants in a safe environment. And you'll have a low-flying bird's eye view, since the overlook is, well, *overlooking* the bears' habitat. Abandoned cubs or injured bears are relocated here, some long-term, others shipped south as soon as they can be rehabilitated.

The Old Pioneer Home is an imposing building in Sitka, situated on nine carefully groomed acres. Formerly a log barracks built by Russians, the people of Sitka saw a need for a safe, home-like place for old pioneers, prospectors, and others who were no longer able to care for themselves. Only indigent men were admitted to the Home in the early years, and when the wooden structure was replaced in 1930, no facilities for women were provided. The 1949 Legislature finally provided funds for a Women's Home and in 1956 the North Wing was added to the main building. Currently close to 170 residents live here. The tiny gift shop is worth a stop. Handicrafts are all made by residents.

With a population of roughly 8,000, Sitka's economy is deeply anchored in its fishing industry and tourism. Residents in ever-present rubber boots frequent stores and restaurants. If you overlook that, they won't raise an eyebrow at your Aloha shirts. In September, Sitka holds its annual "Running of the Boots" festival as a goodbye to its summer visitors and a hello to the returning salmon. It's a quirky sort of place.

Icy Strait Point is located just down the road from Hoonah, and twenty-two miles southeast of Glacier Bay National Park. The place evolved into a lifeline for struggling communities and became a sweet spot for cruise passengers. Struck by a severe downturn in the traditional businesses of fishing and logging, locals glommed onto an alternative source of income, namely tourists. You, in other words.

Icy Strait Point is Alaska Native owned-and-operated, with all monies directly supporting the community of Hoonah, Alaska's largest Native Tlingit village.

Aiming to maintain a place that's man-made but not overly commercialized, only one cruise ship is allowed to dock here per day. Icy Strait offers pretty woodland walks, an insight into Tlingit history and culture, and a wide range of Alaskan. Little craft shops feature native artwork and locally made products. All shops are owned by Alaskans. No "made in China" here.

You can book a tour here, one of twenty or so, or wander on your own, taking in a restored 1912 salmon cannery and museum and quiet nature trails. Keep an eye out for the coastal brown bears that inhabit the area. They were here first. There's even a culinary experience, featuring (you guessed it) salmon. Interested in scaring the daylights out of yourself? Try the zip line, reputed to be the longest and highest in North America. There's no reason to give your guardian angel grey hair, but you may never get back to Alaska. You'd better enjoy it while you're here.

Juneau

In an onboard trivia games, a common question is "Which two US state capitals are not accessible by car?" The answer:

Honolulu and Juneau. It's true; they're both only reachable by sea or air. As you sail into ports, you'll see homes dotting the shoreline, and if you think about it, you'll notice one thing missing from typical American houses. No driveways. Many have a small plane parked beside the house, but cars are not a common way of life in most of Alaska.

Juneau has served as the state capital of Alaska since 1906 when the seat of Alaskan government was moved north from Sitka. Juneau's capital is open for self-guided tours during business hours. It's a surprisingly blocky building, lacking the domed grandeur of some other state capitol buildings. Know why? It was entirely constructed with donations! Alaskans are a thrifty lot.

Juneau sits at sea level, at the Gastineau Channel, with the seaside parts resting on tailings from the old AJ Mine. It's beneath the Juneau Icefield, which feeds more than 30 glaciers. Two glaciers, the Mendenhall Glacier and the Lemon Creek Glacier, are visible from the city proper. While many consider Mendenhall a must-see, and it *is* lovely, the price of reaching the park has more than quadrupled in the last few years. On my last cruise to Alaska, we planned a hike past the glacier to the abandoned gold mine at the top of the waterfall, but balked at the $38 cab ride. That's a lot for a hike.

 Instead, we found a cabbie who said flatly, "I'm boycotting Mendenhall until the fees go down, and I won't take you there. Care for a ride outside of town?" Ah, a kindred spirit! The two-hour private, albeit impromptu, tour was a highlight. The driver was a local resident, a storyteller, and he showed us places tourists never access. Eagle's nests, beaver dams, we looked for bear, watched orca in the harbor off Douglas Island, saw beaver signs, even took a mile-long hike along a silent shore together, and I loved it. Bonus: the Mendenhall Glacier was stunning across the bay, and I could see clear up into the ice field, miles away. That was a perspective I'd missed on previous trips. Sometimes when you stand too close to a sight, you miss the magnificence of it. Mendenhall is beautiful close up, but I won't forget that day anytime soon!

Take time to visit the Alaska State Museum, an especially fine one. For a quirky, low-key site, catch a ride to the Last Chance Mining Museum just outside of town. It's common to see modern-day gold miners in the stream below the museum, complete with hardware store sluices and a bucket. Watch for Galena, the giant benign dog who guards the place. "Galena" is Spanish for "gold," an appropriate name.

Speaking of names, do you know why Juneau isn't named Harrisburg? Well, it was, early on, after Richard Harris. In 1881, the miners met and voted to rename the town Juneau, after prospector Joe Juneau. Okay, there's more to the story than that...Joe Juneau feared the election would be a close one, so the night before election day, he plied voters with copious amounts of beer, then had his team prop half-drunk men up at the polls the next day to vote for him. Won by a landslide...Alaska style.

Valdez is a relatively small city, but it is one of the most important ports in the state, because it's Alaska's northernmost port that stays ice-free all winter. A few cruises stop there. It's the terminus of the Trans-Alaskan Pipeline, the eight-hundred-mile-long pipe that reaches from Fairbanks, transecting the state. The Alaska pipeline museum is an interesting stop. Getting a cruise ship into Valdez requires a 90-degree turn; that alone is worth getting up early to watch. I think our ship missed that oil tanker by mere inches. Valdez is a popular port for tours that head into Prince William Sound for wildlife seekers, kayakers, and fishing.

The original town was severely damaged in a tsunami in the 1960s triggered by the massive Good Friday earthquake. You can still see damage from the quake in Anchorage as well. Valdez town was relocated to a more stable place afterwards.

Oil tankers load crude oil in Valdez, and make their way to points south. I noticed the name of a tanker loading at Valdez, and spotted the same ship ten days later at home, off-loading at one of Puget Sound's refineries! We had similar scenery, but I bet my cruise was more upscale than theirs.

Wildlife

Lion and tigers and bears, oh, my! Not quite, but you can see a wide variety of wildlife in Alaska, and they're not the kind you see in your backyard at home. A sleepy porcupine, a snuffling wild boar, perhaps a bear with her cubs...magical experiences you can't experience anywhere else!

Alaska's seasons are ever changing, and that affects wild things as well. The spring months are prime for spotting moose, maybe even long-legged calves, and Dall sheep as they move down the slopes for better grazing areas. Not many things are cuter than a baby sheep! September is when you're likely to see humpback whales, spawning salmon, and caribou migrating to their winter feeding grounds. In July and August, brown bears fish along the rivers and streams, heedless of tourists. Moose feed around lakes and ponds and along rivers spring throughout the summer. From the ship's vantage point, be on the lookout for seals, porpoises, and dolphins and, of course, don't forget about the whales! Over one thousand humpback whales spend their summers feeding in southeast Alaska, and that doesn't include the other species. They'll take your breath away!

If your cruise line hires a naturalist to be onboard, make friends with him or her as soon as you can. They tend to be well-informed people who love telling about Alaska's wildlife. There's a lot to see, and skilled eyes can help you spot wildlife you might otherwise miss. Wondering why salmon leap into the air, then slap themselves horizontally against the surface of the sea? They know. Is that a humpback whale or a gray, a dolphin or porpoise? Ask away!

Spring (the earlier the better) is a great time to view wildlife because the trees aren't fully in bloom, meaning you can sneak a peek at critters between the branches. Autumn is also good, because animals are fattening up against the long winter, eating everything in sight, and more likely to be in the lowlands as days grow cooler.

Let's look at some common Alaskan residents, the non-human varieties.

Caribou, cousins of deer, live on the Alaska tundra. They're not often seen from ships, but you may see them if you venture inland. Their babies are darling, bouncy little things, like lambs with a spark of mischief. In other places, the terms "caribou" and "reindeer" are used interchangeably. In Alaska, "reindeer" refers exclusively to domesticated caribou. Caribou (or reindeer) are a major source of food for Alaskans, because they're abundant. And tasty.

When my daughter showed photos she'd taken of a reindeer at a park in Alaska, my five-year-old granddaughter said adamantly, "I know all about Santa, and there's no such thing as reindeer. So, what is it?" After several attempts to explain, Daughter gave up and sighed, "Caribou." Five-year-olds can have a stubborn streak. This one's is as wide as her head.

Moose are a gangly creature; as if God had extra pieces left over in the creation and stuck them together into one very large, mild animal. Mild, that is, unless it's baby-having season or mating season; biology waits for no man. Or moose. Cows with calves are fiercely protective, something to keep in mind as you aim your camera. The Alaskan subspecies of moose is the largest in the world, with adult males weighing 1,200 to 1,600 pounds, standing nearly seven feet tall at the shoulder. They appear awkward, but moose can run at speeds of up to 35 mph. The fastest human runners clocked in at 26 miles per hour, and that was a very short distance. The math is not in your favor. Don't antagonize them.

Moose often venture into neighborhoods, casually strolling along city streets. In summer, they frequently wade and swim in lakes and ponds, foraging for tender aquatic plants. Because of the abundance of moose in Alaska, moose-human interactions are frequent. They're brazen, often walking into towns, even up onto porches, if something looks appealing. Flowerboxes are a favorite, and residents don't set pies on the step to cool.

Moose often graze along the state's highways. Moose can sometimes cause problems, standing in the middle of airfields or dangerously crossing the path of cars and trains. They don't seem to know how big they are. Bears and wolves are their main predators, unless you count human hunting. A moose can fill three or four chest freezers against the winter.

Before you mouth off at home about the first moose you've ever seen, you might want to either hold your peace about gender or know what you're talking about. My brother, recently moved from the Midwest, excitedly told a co-worker he'd seen a moose in Alaska. The man replied, "Great! Was it a cow or a bull?"

Confused, Brother said, "It was a *moose*. I'm from Wisconsin. I know what a cow and a bull look like, and this was a *moose*!"

With strained patience, the man slowly asked, "Was it a *boy* moose or a *girl* moose?"

Mountain goats (rock goats) and **Dall sheep** can often be seen throughout the southeastern Alaskan panhandle and along the Cook Inlet near Anchorage. Some have been relocated to Baranof Island, near Sitka, and Kodiak. Constantly on the move, they migrate from the high ridges in the summer and to the treeline in the winter, seeking food. Both goats and sheep are surprisingly agile, climbing to places your mother wouldn't let you go.

Identification can be tricky at a glance, since both are white with split hooves and both favor craggy cliffs. Rock goats have black, curved horns. Dall sheep horns are lighter in color and may curl into full circles. On males, those horns are massive, so big I feel a headache coming on, just looking at them. So much weight for a relatively small body!

How to spot them? Dall lambs are darling, but you're not likely to see them unless you look up, way up, on rocky Alaska cliffs side. Look for off-white spots that move on mountainsides and steep craggy cliffs, and use your binoculars. Dall sheep inhabit all the mountain ranges of Alaska. Mountain goats roam throughout the southeast Panhandle and north and west along the coastal mountains to Cook Inlet.

The only time they venture down from their usual high elevation is when food is scarce; it's not worth the risk from predators usually. If you happen to be driving from Skagway toward Emerald Lake, look up on the high cliffside about a mile from Carcross. See the three Dall sheep?

(How do I know you'll see them? They're fur-covered plywood cut outs!)

Beavers are common in Southeast Alaska, although you're more likely to see evidence of their handiwork than the animals themselves. As you hike, look for young tree stumps gnawed into a point by beaver's bucked teeth. One can fell a five-inch-diameter tree faster than you can tie your hiking boot. Did you know beaver's teeth never stop growing? If they stopped grinding them down by chewing, they'd end up tripping on their own teeth. Beavers dam streams to make ponds deep enough to hide the entrances to their lodges. Lodges look like low mounds of sticks and mud; they're a lot bigger underwater.

Beavers are rodents, but one of the cuter varieties, with rich brown fur and paddle-shaped tails. Beavers live in many of the United States. In Alaska, they're most commonly found from the Yukon northward, and I happen to know there are several dams by Mendenhall Glacier Lake, near Juneau. Because beavers work best underwater, they have secondary eye lids to protect their eyes, and- better yet- ear valves that prevent water from damaging their ears. Ear lids! I've longed for those a few times in my life, haven't you?

Brown bears

Alaska is home to about 70% of the North American brown bear population, with an estimated 30,000 in the state. I don't want to make you paranoid, but even if you can't see a bear, chances are you're quite close to one, no matter where you go in Alaska. Most brown bears are the grizzly type, with the massive Kodiak bears living farther north, near the Aleutian Islands. Alaska also has polar bears, but not where the cruise ships go. Did you know they're Alaska's top predator? Did you further know they have black skin, and their white fur turns green with algae if summer waters are too warm? Amazing, isn't it, the random facts we keep in our heads?

Bears are bold, often scavenging through trash cans, and those huge paws are more agile than you'd think. You'll notice most waste cans in Alaska have bear-thwarting devices, even in cities. Bears hibernate all winter, taking no food or water as their metabolism slows to just above "dead" stage. In the springtime, they're *hungry*. Bears can often be seen scouring stands of dandelions or munching new-growth spruce tips for the much-needed vitamin C.

On another note, dandelions are not native to North America. Early Dutch sailors discovered they felt better when they ate the fast-sprouting leaves (in medical terms, the vitamin C curtailed scurvy symptoms) so packing dandelion seeds on long sea voyages became standard practice. As you know, the seeds fly far and wide on the slightest breeze. Blame the Dutch for the weeds in your yard. Doubtless, hungry bears foraging on bright dandelion patches in the spring appreciate them more than I do!

You grew up thinking teddy bears are cuddly, but that doesn't translate to real ones. Bears can be dangerous; about a dozen serious bear attacks on humans are reported every year. Minor events, such as bears encouraging a startled human to challenge the land-speed record on their way indoors, don't get reported. If you see a bear, your best move is to back away *slowly*.

And make sure you're not between a mama bear and her cubs. Outside of Sitka recently, tourists with cameras edged closer and closer to a mother bear and her twins, causing her to become agitated needlessly. In the words of my three-year-old grandson, she was Noyed. Let them do what they need to do, and use your zoom lens as needed. Remember the goal: have a good time, but stay off the evening news.

Black Bear

The black bear is much smaller than the brown bear, weighing about two hundred pounds in the spring time, and 25% more than that when they head for a winter's nap. Oddly, black bears aren't always black. Colors range from jet black to white, with black being the most common, but don't be surprised to see brown or cinnamon-colored black bears. Besides their size, black bears can be distinguished from brown bears by their claws, which rarely grow more than a couple inches in length.

Muskox haven't changed much since the last ice age. Genetically related to sheep and goats, muskox look more like a buffalo cousin, with massive horns, beards, and long shaggy hair that trails to the ground. Their coat has a coarse outer layer and shorter, very fine underhair. The soft wool-like tufts are gathered in early spring, during shedding season, then spun into yarn, highly prized for its water-resistant warmth and softness.

Mature bulls weigh 600 to 800 pounds, with females weighing close to a third less. When the pack feels threatened, they form a defensive, outward-facing ring with the most vulnerable herd members in the center, much like early pioneers in their covered wagons at rest stops while crossing the plains.

Look for musk oxen grazing on mountain slopes. They often linger along the roadside on the Seward Peninsula, and can be seen on low hillsides as well. Scan for dark spots, then break out your binoculars. They're not great climbers.

In the springtime, their babies bounce and cavort alongside their mothers, acting for all the world like furry toddlers, excited to be alive.

Porcupines are funny-looking creatures, move faster than you might think, and they're thoroughly armed. It's a myth that they can shoot or propel their sharp quills. Still, many a dog with a noseful of needles can attest to the fact that keeping your distance is wise. Quills, covering their body in varying lengths and colors, are modified hairs, hollow, with tiny one-way barbs on the tips. If you decide to pet a porcupine, seek medical help; you'll do more damage if you try to yank the quill out. The quills are used in Native American art and ceremonial dress.

You might find a porcupine in unexpected places, as if one ever starts the day expecting to find a porcupine at all. They crave salt, and several times I've seen them stretched tall, linking the mortar between bricks on buildings! They also eat the glue that bonds plywood together, which isn't always appreciated by whoever built that structure. Porcupines frequently lick the dried human perspiration on hand tools when they get the chance, and even suck up even road salt used to clear streets of snow and ice. Opportunists, porcupines also feed on shed antlers and the bones of dead animals to obtain sodium and calcium. It's a pretty serious craving for them!

Porcupines' habitat is throughout all of Alaska. In wooded areas, porcupines are easy to spot in trees chewing on leaves or waddling across the trail, but you can encounter them just about anywhere, from rocky slopes to tundra meadows, even in backyards and the middle of towns.

Birds

From the funny-looking tufted puffin to the majestic American Bald Eagle, birds of Southeast Alaska are not to be ignored. Many birders call Alaska a prime destination. I like birds well enough, but I've never planned a whole vacation around seeing them. However, South America's penguin population is on my Someday List.

The bald eagle is Alaska's largest resident bird of prey. They're big, with a wing span of up to over seven feet, weighing between eight and fourteen pounds, which is more than you can hold on one finger. They're quick, too, and eagle-eyed is not just a saying. One summer afternoon, I watched an eagle lazily floating on a thermal air current hundreds of feet above a lake. With no warning, it swooped down and grabbed an innocent salmon from the water. Last seen, the hapless fish was struggling in the powerful talons as the bird crested a hill nearby. I suspect the afternoon ended badly for the fish, but I was impressed with the speed and eyesight of the bald eagle!

The bald eagles' iconic white hood and tail don't show up for about five years. If you see a brown-feathered, eagle-shaped bird, it's probably a juvenile. You can also tell by the beak; young eagles have a black beak that later turns yellow. Did you know bald eagles are only found in North America? Forty-nine of the American states: it's too warm in Hawaii for them. And they're more abundant in Alaska than anywhere else in the United States.

The Alaska population is estimated at 30,000 birds. Nesting sites, called aeries, weigh up to 2,000 pounds—a full ton!- and can measure six feet deep. Eagles mate for life and return year after year to add onto the same nest...at least until the tree can no longer support the weight, when the aerie comes crashing down in a storm.

Often, the eagle will choose a likely tree and sit in it for hours, resting and waiting for its next meal to mosey by. Eagles can often be seen along streams during salmon migration times, near canneries, and along docks when the fishing boats come in at the end of a day. If you haven't spotted one yet, try asking a local resident where they've seen one lately. Chances are, it's still there, or not far off.

 In fact, take time to talk with a local resident everywhere you can. They know more than you do, simply by living there. Ask for tips on a good non-touristy restaurant or a site you hadn't even considered, and let them steer you away from a place that sounded great in the brochure, but will be a disappointment once you arrive. Think about it...who knows your hometown better than you? Same in Alaska. Plus, their way of living is likely is quite different than yours. Do *you* spend August at a fish camp, teaching your grandchildren to cut salmon into strips to smoke or dry for the winter? Take time to converse!

The American Bald Eagle is the United States' symbol, adorning its seal, currency, and many legal documents. Did you know it wasn't the first choice? Benjamin Franklin pushed for the lowly turkey buzzard to take its place, insisting, *"For my part, I wish the eagle had not been chosen as the representative of this country. He is a bird of bad moral character; he does not get his living honestly. You may have seen him perched in some dead tree where, too lazy to fish for himself, he watches the labor of the fishing hawk and, when that diligent bird has at length taken a fish and is bearing it to his nest for his young ones, the bald eagle pursues him and takes the fish. With all this injustice, he is never in good case."*

Nevertheless, the bald eagle is a majestic bird, and you'll see many of them on your Alaskan cruise. Watch also for gulls, plovers, osprey, terns, grouse, hawks, puffins, murres, auklets, cormorants and herons as you enjoy your journey. In fact, a good birding book may be just what you need to read while you're counting the days until your cruise.

Sea Creatures and Whales

Besides land-based animals, amazing things inhabit the deep, dark, cold waters of Alaska. Some you may never see from a cruise ship, such as the giant octopus. Others you can spot relatively easily if you look in the right places. Whales top everybody's list, and there's no better place than Alaska to see them in their own home. You may see gray whales, humpbacks, even the mighty blue whales, which make elephants look puny. There are also harbor seals, Stellar sea lions, Minke whales, Pacific white-sided dolphins, Dall's porpoise, harbor porpoise, and cute little sea otters, just for the looking.

I live in northwest Washington, where seeing whales from the coastline is common. I know the whales in Alaska are the exact same whales I saw in Hawaii, Mexico, and Washington, just in a different leg of their migration. I'm not jaded; I'm still amazed every time I see a giant sea mammal, some of the largest animals on earth! Any day that starts with seeing whales before breakfast is destined to be a good day. I've experienced a lot of days like that on cruises in Alaska.

Gray whales migrate to Hawaii in the winter, and make the very long jaunt to Alaska in late April. Did you know that once they begin swimming the four thousand miles or so northbound, the whales don't eat? I like seafood, too, but I sure don't skip meals before I get back to Alaska!

The main thing about whales is...you have to know their patterns, and where and when to look...and you do have to look. My friend who spent six hours every day of her cruise playing Bingo in a windowless theatre never saw a whale, while I saw more than twenty in one morning, right off my balcony.

I spoke to a couple from Pennsylvania who were so excited to go on an expensive whale-watching tour out of Juneau. Later that evening, I asked how they liked the tour. She said she thought she saw two very distant whale spouts against the horizon, but she wasn't sure. That was it: sum total. I didn't have the heart to tell her I'd spent two hours early that morning watching gray whales feeding, including one that performed a full breach, another that spy-hopped, and two that did the repeated-tail-slapping behavior that scientists haven't figured out, plus a pod of orcas and a group of harbor porpoises, all from the glass-walled lounge in the front of the ship. I hate to think of how much she paid for that excursion!

Timing is important. Whales breathe (and thus, surface) all day long, but they tend to feed at dusk and dawn, give or take a couple of hours. If you spot a whale, there are likely others nearby. While whales can hold their breath a very long time, they're still mammals and have to come up for air eventually. When one member of the pod dives, another may spout, so if you see one, keep scanning the horizon.

If you see a few sea birds circling an area of the ocean, head's up! Hungry whales churn up schools of small fish, swimming for their lives, and birds know a dinner-bell opportunity when they see one. If birds are circling, there's a reason. You may even be lucky enough to see whales bubble-net feeding, a cooperative behavior that doesn't end well for the fish.

How do you spot a whale? If you're lucky, one will leap right where you happen to be looking at the right moment. It happens more than you'd guess, if you keep an eye out. Be alert for wisps of mist against the horizon, especially near the mouths of rivers; scan the horizon, where sea meets sky, and watch for plumes. That's probably not mist; it's whales spouting, blowing air and water out of the blowholes on top of their heads before drawing another gulp of air. Once you identify spouting, whales surfacing can't be far behind!

On a cruise to Alaska some time ago, Husband and I were up on deck early with our binoculars, and a pod of humpbacks were putting on a show. There must have been a dozen of them. We phoned his brother to tell him to "Come see! Quick!" Brother rolled out of bed, took a shower, shaved, dressed, stopped at the buffet for a pastry and a cup of hot cocoa, then meandered out on deck. While he complained about the whales being long gone, we headed in for breakfast. Whales often show off, but they do it on their own schedule.

Whales can be playful. On another cruise, as we played shuffleboard on the open promenade deck, three humpbacks kept pace with the ship, not twenty feet from our game. Gorgeous–! They leaped in the spray kicked up by the prow, probably waiting for any snack-sized morsel to be churned up in the water. Husband and I took turns, alternately shooting the shuffleboard game, and hanging over the railing, awed. They were so close, we could smell their fishy breath as they spouted through their blow holes. This went on for over ten minutes, until some "helpful" officer on the bridge announced "Whales! Starboard side," and about three hundred people trampled our game. It's okay, Husband was ahead by several points anyway.

What kind of whales might you see in Alaska?

Beluga whales look unfinished to me, like clean, white play dough, as if the Creator was interrupted during the sculpting process. They can often be seen rolling like beach balls in the Turnagain Passage between Seward and Anchorage. Less commonly, you may spot them near the mouths of rivers. Any place water currents come together, food will be present, and whales know it.

Blue whales are the largest of any mammal, and they can be found in all oceans of the world. I guess when you're that big, you can go where you please. They can grow to eighty feet or more in length, and have been known to startle fisherman looking at their fish finder's screen. *Is that a submarine? A whale?* The blue whales' dorsal fin is set back pretty far on its body; you won't see it until after the massive creature finishes breaching. Don't worry about looking for minute details. If you see a blue whale, you'll know it!

Gray whales feed during the summer along Alaska's Southeast coast, then head south to Mexico or Hawaii for calving season. They have fist-sized bumps on their backs, and tend to collect barnacles. I've seen them surprisingly close to the shoreline in Oregon and Alaska. Anywhere they can find food, there they are, fueling their 24-32-foot bodies.

Humpback whales follow a regular migration route, north to south and back. You're most likely to spot them in the Gulf of Alaska, but keep your eyes out; they can be in Glacier Bay or near the mouth of any river or fjord. They know where the food is. The sure way to identify a humpback is by its knobby dorsal fin. They're show-offs, often flipping their flukes before diving. Did you know every whale's fluke is unique? It's like human fingerprints. Whale-watcher researchers can identify a whale at a glance.

Orca

Large pods (family groups) of orcas frequent Alaskan waters in the summer, up to forty or more together. Females and young ones stay to the center as they swim, with the males surrounding them for protection. Orcas are called "killer whales," but they're not whales at all;

closer related to dolphins. Their reputation of "killer" is accurate, however, sending seals and even birds skittering onto nearby ice floes to save their lives. Orcas are smart, hunting in groups, and dinner-sized creatures don't stand a chance. They eat sea lions, fish, squid, seals, dolphins, and porpoises, and can even attack larger whales when they get the notion.

You might confuse gray whales with humpbacks or dolphins with porpoises, but you can't mistake the distinctive black and white saddle markings on orcas for anything else. Well, most people can't. There was that one passenger on a ship's deck shouting "Orca! Right there! I've *never*!" She still hadn't; that was a log, a plain brown log, floating innocently by.

Male orcas can be as long as a school bus and weigh up to six tons, and they can still swim at twenty-five miles per hour. Their bodies are aerodynamic, designed for speed. Wondering what that glossy skin feels like? Imagine the texture of a wet rubber inner tube; that's pretty close.

Minke whales are smaller, about twenty feet in length at maturity. They're named for a Captain Minke who was known to greatly exaggerate, insisting the variety of whale he saw was "*THIS BIG!*" As your mother told you, bragging will get you nowhere. In worst-case scenarios, it can lead to a whale species being named after you. Minkes tend to be solitary, unless there's a baby Minke nearby. They're dark grey to black in color, with a white band on the top side of their pectoral fins. They range across the northwest Pacific Ocean, and every corner of Alaskan waters.

Have you heard the phrase, "scarcer than hen's teeth"? Even more scarce are whales' teeth. You'd think, for a creature that size, they'd have enormous teeth, but most have none at all. Orcas are one exception. Others strain their food through baleen, long, tough, layered strands of keratin, the same stuff your fingernails are made of. Alaskan whales filter tiny plankton, krill, shrimp, and small fish, even chasing schools of sardines, anchovies, cod, herring, and capelin with their mouths open. And oddly, small whales have the same diet as blue whales. If you assumed big whales eat big fish, you're mistaken.

Dolphins and Porpoises

Whales are undeniably spectacular, but there's plenty of other fascinating sea creatures to admire. I'm partial to dolphins. On an early cruise to Alaska, I was standing on the aft of the ship, soaking in the scenery on both sides of the Inside Passage, knowing the cruise would end in Vancouver the following day. A Pacific white-sided dolphin leaped, then another, then dozens and hundreds! A passing crew member said, "There they go again. Every week, like clockwork." He explained that's where the ship discharged the food waste, now ground to a fine pulp, and the dolphins were attuned to the ship's engine signature. Like a dinner bell, rung for dolphins. I'm not sure I like the idea of spewing food waste into the sea that close to land, but the dolphins begged to differ.

People often confuse porpoises with dolphins, but the two come from distinctly different families. Dolphins usually have pointy beaks and more noticeable dorsal fins. Porpoises are usually smaller without the pronounced melons or beaks. That's how to tell if it's a dolphin or porpoise at a glance: porpoises' noses are more blunt.

Dolphins are a lot of fun to watch. They're very acrobatic, often pacing the ships and playing in the spray from the ship's wake. They enjoy company, often seen in groups of twenty or more.

Dall porpoises' markings resemble orcas, and they're nearly as fast as the killer whales, but much smaller, averaging six feet long and tipping the scales at three hundred pounds. They're easy to spot from a ship due to a preferred behavior called "bow riding." The bow of a moving ship creates a pressure wave in the water; imagine the whoosh of wind after a big truck passes. Porpoises and dolphins sidle up to a boat and swim just below the surface, riding in the pressure wave, and it looks like they enjoy it.

If you spot a porpoise in calm seas gently leaping with graceful rolling motions, you've likely found a harbor porpoise. They're about a hundred twenty pounds, grey or dark brown, with much smaller dorsal fins than other dolphins. Watch them awhile; it's good for the soul to observe Nature going about her business.

Steller Sea Lion

The "Lion of the Sea" earned its name because of its distinctive bellowing roar. Seriously foul-tempered things, they smell just terrible, as if they haven't bathed in years, which is pretty funny, if you think about it. They spend much of their time in the ocean, after all. Males can reach eleven feet in length and weigh more than a ton. Out of the water, sea lions look like big brown beanbag chairs, but in the water, they're graceful, almost elegant. I watched one surfing on waves crashing onto a beach one afternoon, riding one after another, over and over. Minus the surfboard.

Harbor Seal

Harbor seals are mammals, not fish, but they seem to be designed to function better in water than on land. They're wobbly and blubbery and can't outrun anybody. They tend to congregate in groups for their protection. Watch for harbor seals on icebergs and the buoys that mark the way for boats into harbors. The clanging doesn't seem to bother them.

Sea Otters

 I like the otters' sense of optimism. Every morning, each otter selects a rock, their favorite rock, and sets it on its chest. The rock is about the size of a toddler's fist, and there it stays, all day. While the otter floats lazily on its back, the rock doesn't move. If the otter spies dinner, perhaps a clam or oyster or sea urchin, the rock is swiftly clenched in its paw, and use to smash open the delicacy. After lunch, the rock goes back on the otter's chest, ready for the next snack to appear. I like the sense of hopefulness: *Surely I'll find food today.*

Adult sea otters weigh about one hundred pounds, making them the heaviest members of the weasel family, but among the smallest marine mammals. They're cuter than regular weasels, and larger than river otters.

Salmon is king in Alaska. Nearly every river and stream that reaches to the sea is a natural spawning ground for one kind of salmon or another. Salmon from some rivers are extra-special, or extra-specially marketed, at least. When the salmon from the Copper River in Alaska reach grocery stores, plan on paying a hefty price tag! They're only available for a few short days.

The main varieties of salmon are Chinook salmon (King), Red salmon (sockeye), Silver salmon (Coho), Pink salmon (humpback, humpy, or pinks) and Chum. Salmon lovers can identify the nuances of each with one bite.

Chinook or King salmon is a great-tasting fish and can weigh more than 40 pounds. The Chinook salmon's large size and high-quality flesh makes it one of Alaska's most valuable commercial products, as well as luring in sport fishers (and their cash) from all over the world. It's also Alaska's state fish. I have no idea what my state's favorite fish is; it's not a fact I keep in my mind. May, June, and July are the best times for King salmon fishing in Alaska's rivers and streams, although they can be caught year-round. An oily fish, King salmon has a rich, almost buttery, flavor. It's excellent served as tartare. That's finely diced raw fish, not *tartar*, the mayonnaise-based condiment. Both have their place, but they're certainly not interchangeable.

Silver or Coho salmon are the second-largest of Alaska's salmon. High quality Coho salmon are often frozen whole and sold as a delicacy in markets across Asia, Europe, and North America. It's delicious grilled, baked, or smoked. Smoked salmon in any flavor or form is wonderful stuff spread on crackers or in chowder. Or on a fork, for that matter; no fancy recipe required. Coho are extremely important to Alaska's economy in the form of attracting sport fishermen, both in marine and freshwater systems. Those fisher-tourists add to the local economy in the form of meals, lodging, and equipment, including yet another lost reel. Coho are easy to catch, but they put up a fight. I can't blame them.

Red or Sockeye salmon have brilliant scarlet flesh that's just plain pretty on a dinner plate. Add a little dill, and it's also delicious. Fly fishermen reserve their spot at fishing lodges months or years in advance, hoping to land their limit of sockeyes. Although more chum and pink salmon are commercially caught, sockeye salmon are a higher quality fish and thus bring in more money on the market. Somewhat milder than other salmon, many people insist sockeye is the best tasting out of all types of salmon. Me included - it's my favorite, with a little lemon and parsley...mmmm. It's also the best variety for lox, a velvety, lightly smoked salmon often served on bagels with thinly sliced onions.

Pink or Humpy salmon are the smallest of the five types of salmon, averaging 3-5 pounds. With a soft flesh and fishy-er flavor, they're not for everybody, but they're good smoked or canned. The humpy is the most abundant (by far!) of all salmon in Alaska with annual commercial catches exceeding 140 million. Almost all commercially caught pink salmon is canned. Pink salmon are called humpies because adult males develop an enormous hump behind the head, along with a strange-looking hooked head, as they mature. Huge numbers of pink salmon spawn in Ketchikan's streams late in the season, and with that ominous hump, they're frankly a little scary-looking.

Chum salmon used to be reserved mainly for sport fishermen, but in the last few years, they've been commercially harvested, mostly for the Japanese and European markets. Chum salmon is a very dry fish, best eaten in chowders or as jerky. It's not a good sandwich-with-cole-slaw fish, no matter how carefully you prepare it.

What To Pack

Sure, you're a traveler; you know how to pack for a trip, right? Hold your proverbial horses! Packing for Alaska is unlike packing for any other cruise. In the Caribbean, a carry-on bag containing a couple of swimsuits, sandals, a broad-brimmed hat and sundresses is fine for a week. Add in sunblock and sunglasses and you're good to go. Not so in Alaska; forget about packing light for the Great Land. Temperatures and weather systems swing wildly in Alaska. In a week-long cruise, you could walk on a glacier, get sunburned on a fishing boat, hike in 75 degree weather and encounter snow flurries on the way back to the ship - and yes, bring a swimsuit because swimming in a cruise ship's pool in a glacier-lined fjord is just a cool thing to do.

As I taught my kids, figure out what you'll be doing in a given day and be sure to pack what you need for the occasion. If the day includes a swim in the ship's pool, a hike on an ice field, shopping, and a nice dinner, pack accordingly. In this case, you'd want a swimsuit, long pants and a warm coat, good shoes, and a dressy outfit. Closed-toed shoes are best for anything but a trek to the pool. You don't want to bark your toe on uneven paths, flip flops simply don't work on ice, and many shore excursions require actual shoes.

Packing isn't hard; just bring what you need. I overheard a man berating a Guest Services agent on an Alaskan cruise. Seemed he was freezing, and it was all their fault, in his eyes. All he'd packed were tee shirts and Bermuda shorts because "Everyone knows cruises are warm!" I'm pretty sure the agent was rolling his eyes internally, but he kept a straight face.

On glacier-watching day on a recent Alaskan cruise, we met a young woman on the bow of the ship. Everyone around her was wearing parkas, gloves, hats, scarves, and goosebumps, but she flaunted denim shorts and tee with flip flops. It gets very windy on the bow, and we were in a glacial fjord, after all. She boasted loudly about how she never gets cold. As the ship eased closer to the glacier, I noticed her face turn red, then white, and somebody gave her a wool pool blanket, then her nose looked blueish to me and she finally slipped indoors, no longer speaking. I saw her the next day in town, where it was about 70 degrees, wearing a heavy jacket with an Alaskan logo and furry boots. Apparently, she'd been shopping!

The key to being comfortable in Alaska is dressing in layers. You might need a jacket in the morning and short sleeves in the afternoon. Be sure to bring a waterproof (not just water-resistant) jacket. Don't forget that most of coastal Alaska is temperate rainforest. Plan on encountering drizzle or rain, unless you're very lucky. On our very first cruise to Alaska, we had sunny days in every port, without a single raindrop. And in every single port, people marveled at how lucky we were, insisting, "It's been raining for weeks, except today, and more rain is forecast tomorrow." I like serendipity.

Southeast Alaska is partly a rain forest, a fact I've reminded you of repeatedly, because it's important to keep in mind when you're making your packing list. If you're expecting clear sunny skies the whole cruise, you're probably out of luck. On the other hand, at least twice when I was in Ketchikan on a cruise, I needed sunblock more than my rain jacket, as temperatures rose to over 80 degrees with nary a cloud in the sky. Did I mention Alaska's weather in unpredictable? Layers, I tell you!

And it's a good idea to waterproof your walking shoes to keep your feet comfy and dry. Be aware that it can be really chilly near glaciers, even on sunny days. Dress warmly, and add a hat and gloves. You don't want to have to retreat indoors and miss the show just because your goosebumps are piling up.

Tuck a few disposable ponchos in your pocket or bag. They're not fashionable, but you'll be a lot more comfortable protected from a thick drizzle or an outright downpour. They're extremely small and light. You can buy them in every port as well as onboard most ships, for several times the cost of picking them up ahead of time. Dollar stores sell them in three-packs. Don't plan on using them more than once; they don't last. Reminds me of the time in Spain, when a sudden downpour left us drenched during a walking tour. Out came yesterday's ponchos. With a few rips and a couple of strategic knots, I made do, but I studiously avoided mirrors all day. Plan on a fresh one.

Don't take an umbrella. It rains frequently in Southeast Alaska, but umbrellas are practically useless. It'll be in the way on sidewalks, you risk impaling other tourists, you'll feel silly hiking a wilderness trail with one, and the capricious wind tends to grab umbrellas and turn them inside out, just for fun. All you need is a lightweight waterproof jacket, preferably with a hood. I'm from the

Seattle area, and I don't ever use an umbrella. I admit I keep one in my car because my mother insists on it (you have a mother, too, right?) but for people around here – and in Alaska - it's a matter of pride. We wear a lot of waterproofed jackets, many Gore-Tex items, but umbrellas are ...simply beneath us.

I'm not a fan of bulky clothing. In my case, I disdain thick, furry parkas in favor of layers. A shirt, sweater or fleece top, jeans, and jacket are plenty, with thermal underwear if the day involves playing in snow or walking on ice. I add a hat, although hats are not good with my curls. If you get too warm, simply shed enough clothes to make yourself comfortable.

Even on a warm day, sometimes the wind kicks up across the ocean, and that cold wind will go right through you. Whoever said 70 degrees is hot never stood on the open deck of a moving cruise ship. I favor wraps and pareo. I take those wherever I travel, no matter the climate. They're great for blocking wind or overly aggressive air conditioning onboard, and they can dress up any outfit. Cardigans also work.

Synthetic hiking pants are a good option; the zip-off legs come in handy if the weather warms. Silk underwear is light, but surprisingly warm. A polar fleece top can come on and off in a moment, and they're lightweight, warm, and wad up easily in the corner of a suitcase. I'm not a fan of clothes that wrinkle when I travel. Or anywhere else, for that matter. I don't own any linen attire. It can wrinkle just by me looking at it!

Some cruise lines give passengers a ship-logo tote bag. These are known as Sell-Me-Something bags in town, marking you as an inexperienced tourist. A better idea is to bring a lightweight daypack to stash your layers as you shed them throughout the day, along with any purchases you might make. Save the tote bag for showing-off purposes at home, along with the ship-logo coaster, deck of cards, and any pens you may have filched from the purser's office.

While ships tend to be moving away from the starchy former formality of yesteryear, some still require a dress up night or two. Others call it optional. Read up on your particular cruise line's requirements, of course. Overall, Alaska isn't a dressy place; it just isn't. While some passengers opt for ball gown and tux, you'll be fine in a dressy top and nice slacks or skirt for women, perhaps a simple cocktail dress if you feel ambitious, and a collared shirt (with or without a tie) for men. With having to pack warm clothing, you'll likely find bringing your sequins and suit coat is more trouble than they're worth. However, if this is your one and only chance to dress to the nines all year, by all means, ignore me. And take lots of pictures.

I travel rather a lot, and I know shoes can make or break a trip. On old cobblestones, slippery trails, or while scaling yet another lighthouse, I don't want to wear wobbly shoes that invite a turned ankle. When I'm on the go, I opt for sturdy walking shoes: nonskid, light-weight, cushy, and flexible. I want to be free to explore without sore feet. High heels are impracticable on a moving cruise ship, more so if the motion of the ocean sways the ship to any degree. Even the onboard performers, who are used to wild waves, switch out their fancy dancing heels for flats if the ship's rolling much at all. They do; pay attention next time!

Wear comfortable shoes with good soles for hiking and walking around town, as well as climbing in and out of boats as needed. Some shore tours require closed-toe shoes, such as zip lining and river rafting trips. At the least, you'll be warmer on glaciers, muddy trails, sidewalks, and wherever else your feet take you.

Unless they're your daily footwear of choice, skip the hiking boots. I haven't worn hiking boots since that trip across Michigan years ago, where I walked fifty-six miles in a long weekend, cutting a trail with the Sierra Club. When I finally made it home, I retired my heavy hiking boots and framed backpack in favor of sturdy walking shoes and a lightweight day pack. And I now carry a compass when needed. Those fifty-six miles were intended to be closer to forty-four!

 Make sure any shoes you pack are comfortable. Going from shoe store to four-mile hike in shoes that don't fit quite right is just asking for blisters. Blisters are tiny things, but the agony they trigger is anything but tiny. Dry socks are a must; pack a couple pair more than you plan on needing. Do buy some of that waterproof spray from the shoe store, and use it liberally before you pack, at least a couple of layers. On a drizzly day, you'll thank me. Wet feet are no fun, and why ruin a pair of decent shoes? Those cute patterned rain boots are awfully clunky after a few steps. They're going to be more annoying than helpful for a day in port.

Bring an extra pair of shoes in case the first pair gets wet, just in case.

And, as a further tip, I suggest packing them yourself. I bought new shoes for a recent cruise; pretty, comfortable, versatile; exactly what I needed for the trip. They, plus the ones on my feet, were the only shoes I planned on. The cruise was only a quick, four-day jaunt, after all. I chose a much smaller suitcase than Husband's, and he said, "If you need to put something in mine, just set it on the bed." I left the pair of new shoes and an alarm clock with his stuff to pack.

In San Diego, I was baffled to find only one of my shoes and no clock. Who packs *one* shoe? I found it on the floor at home when we returned. I guess it had slipped off the bed, but I still think he should have asked if I really intended to bring both shoes. Does he think I hop? Remember to pack an even number of shoes.

Bring binoculars! Bring one for each of you; there's nothing more frustrating than missing that whale spy hop or the glacier face calving because your partner elbowed you in the ribs to get a turn. I like opera glasses because they're small and lightweight, but the big zoom versions are certainly great, if you don't mind hauling them around. A good camera with more SD cards or film than you think you'll possibly use is a good idea, too. A tip: most cruise lines show the day of the week in the elevator, perhaps in carpeting or a tag of some sort. Take a picture of this first thing every day, and your photos will automatically be sorted.

Snow and ice reflects more sunlight than city-dweller eyes can take in. In extreme cases, called snow blindness, you can temporarily damage the color rods in your eyes, rendering everything you see black and white, if you can see at all. Polarized sunglasses allow you to see much clearer, while preventing eye strain and swelling. You'd be amazed at how many more spawning salmon you can see in that rushing stream once the glare is cut by decent sunglasses! And if you're not squinting, you may even spot a baby porcupine trailing his mama. That's not something you see every day at home.

Bring insect repellant. Double check to be sure it's packed. Mosquitos are said to be Alaska's state bird, and they're not kidding. My daughter complained mightily when the little beggars repeatedly wriggled between her eyes and the binocular lenses. Sometimes, that faint cloud on the horizon isn't made of water droplets at all. Save some itching; grab the repellant!

Sunscreen is also a good idea to avoid sunburn, and I recommend some sort of lotion or cream for your face. Standing the bow with the wind whipping can sting, and who needs chapped cheeks? Lip balm can be your friend, too.

Many cruisers and tourists consider Alaska a bucket list destination, but why wait until the end of your life to experience such a spectacular place? What are you waiting for?

The End

If you're in the mood for an Alaska cruise novel to get you in the mood for your fabulous trip, read *Murder On Deck* today!

Please take time to read my other cruise books. You'll find *Tips From The Cruise Addict's' Wife* And *More Tips From The Cruise Addict's Wife* especially helpful as you plan your once-in-a-lifetime Alaskan cruise! Loaded with tips and tricks designed to save you a boatload of money on any cruise, you'll know more than anybody on the ship! (except the captain, who earned that place)

Please head over and **leave a review** on Amazon.com.

Reviews mean more than you know!

Other Books by Deb Graham

Murder On Deck   *a cruise novel*

Peril In Paradise   *a cruise novel*

Tips From The Cruise Addict's Wife

More Tips From The Cruise Addict's Wife

Mediterranean Cruise With The Cruise Addict's Wife

How To Write Your Story

How To Complain...*and get what you deserve*

Hungry Kids Campfire Cookbook

Kid Food On A Stick

Quick and Clever Kids' Crafts

Awesome Science Experiments for Kids

Savory Mug Cooking

Uncommon Household Tips

Excerpt from Tips From The Cruise Addict's Wife:

The couple staying in the penthouse cabin will be sitting at the same table, eating the same wonderful foods, visiting the same ports of call, seeing the same shows, and experiencing the same things as you. **They'll just be paying anywhere from 5 to 15 times what you'll pay.** Another way to look at it is ... *they'll* take one cruise, and for the same cost *you'll* be able to take 15 cruises! Do you really need a butler?

If you have a penthouse or even a full suite, you'll find you spend more time in it. You may not go to shows, or even restaurants, content to order room service...again. If you have a smaller cabin, you'll spend more time out and about, enjoying the ship's features, meeting interesting people, dining in new places. It's up to you---personally, I'm ON A SHIP, so I don't want to feel confined to a room, like in a hotel, even if the confinement is of my own choosing.

My brother's family went on a Hawaiian cruise a year before our family took the same cruise; same ship, same itinerary. He paid over $10,000 for the penthouse suite. For a *Week!* We spent $1900, for three of us, and booked an inside cabin, planning to spend our money in ports, exploring. We were upgraded to a balcony cabin for $190 (total!) just a week before the cruise. I know for a fact we had more fun than my brother's family!

Cabin prices are based on double occupancy. **Solo passengers pay a surcharge**, often 200%. You're better off finding a friend or family member to pay half the cost of the cabin. You do have a friend, right?

Inside Cabins

Inside cabins have a bad rap. Think about it; if they were as bad as you have heard, how could the cruise lines possibly sell out, cruise after cruise? Unless you are claustrophobic, inside **cabins are just fine**. If you are, you probably should consider a balcony upgrade an unavoidable medical expense, and do what you gotta do.

Inside cabins are well laid out and efficient. Many people rave about how they sleep better in total darkness. They are often quieter, too, depending on location. The main selling point, of course, is the price. They often cost much much less than same-sized cabins with a porthole or window.

On much older ships, I admit, I would have been miserable in an inside cabin. I've heard stories from decades ago about one passenger having to step out into the hall so the other person could open the bathroom door. And some standard two-person cabins even had full -on bunk beds! I enjoy camping as much as the next person, but my soul balks at the idea of taking off my sequined dress to climb into a bunk bed. The key to this paragraph is "decades ago." You'd have to look far and wide for conditions this tight on modern ships.

A nice feature of an inside cabin is the total darkness. Great for sleeping! It can be a little disorienting in the morning, when you're not sure what time it is or is it daylight yet. Before you go to sleep, **turn the TV tuned to the channel with the "bridge cam" or "view from the bridge," with the sound off.** You'll have a window to the world when the sun comes up.

Inside cabins are always smoke-free. Smoke can drift over from a nearby balcony, but if you're especially sensitive, an inside cabin is your best bet.

Families *can* fit in an inside cabin --- we've done it with two teenagers---but you have to really like them. We like ours. Rather than book a slightly larger Family Suite, **consider two inside cabins**, nearby or adjacent. It'll cost less, you'll appreciate having the extra bathroom, and they sometimes stay neater, too. Well, ours did...we booked a Girl Cabin and a Boy Cabin, with the appropriate gender parent and kid in each. The Girl Cabin was tidy all week. The Boy Cabin looked like something had exploded, and it was wearing a lot of clothing at the time.

Check the Deck

Before you decide on a cabin, **look at deck plans above and below the cabin you are considering.** Extra noisy places include under the pool deck (staff drags out deck chairs at dawn), by the anchor, near the teen club, and above the theatre and nightclub. People tend to shy away from cabins near elevators, but we've found them to be quiet. Elevators tend to be separated from corridors by a fire wall, which acts as a sound barrier.

Cabins with non-opening windows can be designated Ocean View, Obstructed, or Partially Obstructed. Again, **examine the deck plans, and those above and below the cabin you're considering.** Some obstructions can be minimal, such as a lifeboat hanging high above the window, or you may only be able to see a tiny slice of the ocean if you crane your neck very far to the left while standing on the bed. Decide if the cost is worth it to you.

If you opt for a balcony cabin, be sure to **check the deck plan before you book.** Some cabins are open at the top, unprotected from sun and rain. Worse, people above can look right down on you; not very private! Cove or Hull balconies are towards the front of the ship, where it curves. They can be enclosed partway up, or blocked on both sides by a solid frame, limiting your view a bit. The advantage is that some of the wind is also blocked, but of course, so is the view. Just be aware of what you're getting. Try doing an online search for that specific cabin number; people post pictures of just about everything.

A major complaint about balcony cabins is that cigarette smoke wafts over into neighboring balconies, or cabins, when the door is open. It's not a problem for the occasional cigarette...you just wait them out, but a cabin of three chain smokers can make your balcony unusable. **Smoking policy varies by cruise line**, so read up on yours.

Smoking on ships is a heated topic, and cruise line policies vary greatly. If your balcony adjoins that of a smoker, a **small battery operated fan** can prevent murder at sea, or at least increase the time you can enjoy your balcony without fumes wafting over.

Before you book a balcony cabin, **consider your destination's weather.** A balcony is a sweet treat in warm climates. How much time will you spend out there in the cold rain? Our first balcony cabin kept me awake; the door banged at every gust of wind! In Hawaii, we spent considerable time on the balcony.

If your cabin has a window or balcony, **be aware of your location at all times.** There have been numerous stories of people being intimate on their balconies, in full view of those on shore. Did you know passengers can be <u>fined</u> for that in some places?

Our ship was just pulling into Halifax early one morning. I came out of the shower, wearing the appropriate attire for that activity, my birthday suit, and realized with a start that Husband had opened the curtains. I was shocked to see a worker on the dock, not ten feet from our cabin, eye level and looking right at me! He was also surprised, but he did manage a jaunty wave before I snatched the curtains shut.

We just don't spend enough time in the cabin to justify the higher cost of an expensive cabin. Mostly, we use it to sleep, shower, change clothes, and regroup. I enjoy being out and about on the ship. You can sit in a hotel room anywhere!

Please head over and **_leave a review_** on Amazon.com.

Reviews mean more than you know!

Made in the USA
Columbia, SC
08 July 2022